To dear [...]

With m[...]

& many [...]

those 'Mr Darcy' conversations
at the kitchen table!

Amanda x
2013

FINDING Mr DARCY

Amanda Hooton was born and brought up in Western Australia. At nineteen, she moved to Scotland to attend St Andrews University, where she lived at the same college as Prince William (some years, alas, before he arrived). Having studied the great career-oriented degree of Medieval History and English, she used her extensive knowledge of King Arthur and the Knights of the Round Table to secure a fortnight's work experience at *The Scotsman* newspaper in Edinburgh, and spent two years there before moving to the *Daily Telegraph* in London. She returned to Australia in 1999, and has been a staff journalist at *Good Weekend Magazine,* with the *Sydney Morning Herald* and *The Age* newspapers, ever since. She has won both a Walkley award for Australian journalism and a British Press Award.
Finding Mr Darcy is her first book.

Some of the people in this book have had their names changed to protect their identities.

First published 2012 in Macmillan by Pan Macmillan Australia Pty Limited
1 Market Street, Sydney

Copyright © Amanda Hooton 2012

The moral right of the author has been asserted.

All rights reserved. No part of this book may be reproduced or transmitted by any person or entity (including Google, Amazon or similar organisations), in any form or by any means, electronic or mechanical, including photocopying, recording, scanning or by any information storage and retrieval system, without prior permission in writing from the publisher.

National Library of Australia
Cataloguing-in-Publication data:

Hooton, Amanda.

Finding Mr Darcy : Jane Austen's guide to dating
for the modern girl / Amanda Hooton.

9781742611846 (hbk.)

Dating (Social customs)
Courtship

646.77

Internal text design by Allison Colpoys
Typeset in 11.75/17.75 pt Adobe Garamond by Post Pre-press Group
Printed by McPherson's Printing Group

Papers used by Pan Macmillan Australia Pty Ltd are natural, recyclable products made from wood grown in sustainable forests. The manufacturing processes conform to the environmental regulations of the country of origin.

CONTENTS

Introduction 1
Jane Austen: The Novels 5

1 Be Nice 17
2 Be Humorous 23
3 Be Clever 29
4 Be Beautiful 35
5 The Hero 43
6 The Bastards 49
7 Go Where the Boys Are 59
8 The First Move 67
9 Stand Still and Smile 75
10 Feminine Wiles 83
11 The Wingman 91
12 The Phonecall 97
13 When He Doesn't Call 105
14 The First Date 113
15 Sex 121
16 Gay or Straight 129
17 The New Relationship 135
18 Making Love Last 141
19 The Patchwork of Happiness 147
20 Don't Panic 155

21	The Devastating Silence	163
22	Marriage	169
23	Babies	177
24	The Hideous Break-up	183
25	Staying Friends – Hah!	189
26	Preserve Your Dignity	197
27	Not Every Man is Mr Darcy	205
28	A Brilliant Career	215
29	Money Isn't Everything	223
30	Life Without a Mr Darcy	231

Acknowledgements 237

For Dom
who is even cooler than Mr Darcy

*We fall in love the way we do because
we learned it from literature.*

– Anonymous

INTRODUCTION

It is a truth universally acknowledged that finding a decent man – in any place, during any period, and while wearing any variation of empire-line muslin or thigh-high leather – is pretty much the most difficult task an enterprising heroine can set herself. You can have everything else in your life completely sorted: good job, great hair, a beautiful tank full of Siamese fighting fish that you've persuaded to live in a spirit of perfect harmony rather than tearing each other fin from undulating fin; but none of that ensures that you will also have in your possession a lovely man with a slow smile and dark hair that falls over the edge of his collar.

The brutal reality is that meeting your soulmate is hard work. It can be frustrating, disappointing, confidence-sapping, and, often, totally confusing, because it's different from accomplishing anything else in your life. It's not something you can achieve by simple desire; otherwise we'd all be going out with Brad Pitt or George Clooney, depending only on our preferences for dark/blond Lake Como/New Orleans. Nor, for that matter, can you make it happen by sheer force of will. Unlike a career, romance will not yield to application and hard work and strategic planning and going into the office on weekends. (Though if you *do* go into the office on the weekend, who knows? Perhaps you might finally end up at the coffee machine at the same time as that lovely guy in accounts who you always *suspected* was cute, and My God, now you've seen him in jeans and a grey marle T-shirt there can no possible room for doubt.) Nor can you ensure it by being a good person and repaying your karmic debt and generally being at one with the universe – witness the enormous number of, I'm sorry, total bitches who have boyfriends (so many, indeed, that one is sometimes forced to wonder if *being* a bitch is not in fact a prerequisite for *getting* a boyfriend) and the equally enormous number of lovely, kind, gorgeous girls who don't.

That's why you need this book. Because if there's one great truth of life, love, and literature, it's this:

EVERYTHING YOU NEED TO KNOW ABOUT LOVE YOU CAN LEARN FROM JANE AUSTEN. *EVERYTHING.*

INTRODUCTION

That's what this book is about: meeting the modern-day Mr Darcy, and drawing him into your convulsive grasp on a more or less permanent basis. Of course, there are lots of other books out there that deal with this topic. But this one has a secret weapon – the literary equivalent of a guided missile, able to obliterate its opponents from a thousand miles with the mere touch of a button. It has Jane Austen, and Jane Austen's Rules for Love.

Jane was born in 1775 and died (at only 41) in 1817. She lived through the French Revolution, the Declaration of Independence, and the madness of King George. And she knew, long before Diana Ross did, that love don't come easy. She knew the Game of Love was one of high art and low cunning, of rose-tinted fantasy and clear-eyed realism, of surrendering to the moment and keeping your wits about you. And she knew, too, that hard as it is, it really is the only game in town.

So gird yourself. If you really want a man – and not just any man, but a proper Jane Austen hero (albeit without the lace cuffs or the skin-tight pantaloons – though, who knows? Skin-tight pantaloons might in certain circumstances have quite a bit going for them), take heart. The aim of this book is to give you, gentle reader, thirty of Jane's rules for meeting Mr Darcy, falling in love, and living happily ever after. Huzzah!

JANE AUSTEN: THE NOVELS

Just in case life, the universe and the immoderate consumption of vodka has interfered with your reading or recall of Jane Austen's novels, here's a quick run-down of the major people, plot lines, and romance imperatives of the great sextet.

PRIDE AND PREJUDICE
Hero: *Mr Fitzwilliam Darcy – of course, of course, of course*
Heroine: *Miss Elizabeth Bennet – who else?*

This is Jane's extraordinary, eternal hit, the epicentre of the Austen universe. Basically, it's about Elizabeth Bennet and Mr Darcy as they meet each other, scorn each other, become completely preoccupied with each other and, lo and behold, fall for each other. Other players include Elizabeth's lovely older sister **Jane Bennet**, who loves Darcy's best friend **Mr Bingley**; Elizabeth's slapper younger sister **Lydia Bennet**, who runs off with ne'er-do-well soldier **George Wickham** (who Elizabeth herself quite fancies for a while – for shame, Lizzie!), and Elizabeth's friend **Charlotte Lucas**, who marries the unbelievably appalling **Mr Collins**. Notable events include Elizabeth refusing Mr Collins, refusing Mr Darcy (!!!!), and visiting Mr Darcy's massive country pile in Derbyshire, Pemberley, with her very nice uncle and aunt Gardiner (during which the endless French windows, curving staircases and sweeping emerald lawns in no way soften her view of Darcy – not remotely). Then Lydia runs off with Wickham, Darcy rescues the Bennet family from subsequent disgrace, Elizabeth gets into a slanging match with Darcy's aunt (**Lady Catherine de Burgh**) amongst the shrubbery, and everything comes right in the end, thanks to a bracing walk down a country lane. This is Jane's happiest, funniest, and most straightforward novel: a total joy from start to finish.

EMMA
Hero: *Mr Knightley*
Heroine: *Emma Woodhouse*

Another huge hit. Emma Woodhouse is the much-loved, extremely competent, but occasionally rather smug younger daughter of lovely old hypochondriac Mr Woodhouse. She runs her father's house, and, when the novel opens, is slightly like a young Margaret Thatcher: accustomed to the habit of command. Mr Knightley is her neighbour and old friend, and the only person in the district remotely capable of: a) standing up to her, and b) knocking her down to size. The plot involves this pair coming to realise, through various terribly English trials and tribulations (picking strawberries, painting portraits, organising carriages on snowy evenings) that not only are they great mates and sparring partners, they also completely adore each other. Alongside the main narrative are various side stories, which basically involve Emma bossing everybody about and trying to make them do what she thinks they should do, and love who she thinks they should love – always the wrong thing and the wrong person. First she tries to sool her protégé, orphan **Harriet Smith**, who's in love with Knightley's protégé, farmer **Robert Martin**, onto a hideous social-climbing reverend called **Mr Elton**. Then she spends ages flirting with local rich boy **Frank Churchill**, and being slightly arch and cruel about impoverished beauty **Jane Fairfax**, totally oblivious to the fact that Frank and Jane are secretly in love. The only people she doesn't misjudge, in fact, are her lovely ex-governess **Mrs Weston** (nee Taylor) – who has recently left the Woodhouses to marry Frank's cheerful dad **Mr Weston** – and Mr Knightley. Tellingly, these two are also the only two who see through all her nonsense, and truly love her. After a nightmarish moment among the strawberries where she's thoughtlessly scornful to kind, foolish **Miss Bates**, and Knightley tears a strip off her, Emma takes a long hard look at herself, realises she's been behaving like a (well-bred, reasonably refined) nightmare, and resolves to reform. And while Emma's in the grip of this epiphany, Mr Knightley is simultaneously realising he loves her. All is revealed, and resolved, amongst the shrubbery. (Shrubbery and/or the confidential possibilities of country lanes, you should be realising, play an important part in the love lives of Jane Austen heroines.)

SENSE AND SENSIBILITY
Hero(es): *Edward Ferrars, Colonel Brandon*
Heroine(s): *Elinor Dashwood, Marianne Dashwood*

Jane's version of the double-header, and her third mega-hit. When the novel begins, older sister Elinor – a lovely, calm person – is in love with a young clergyman called **Edward Ferrars**, and soon afterwards, her younger sister Marianne – a drama queen – manages to plunge down a hill in the rain, be rescued by, and become infatuated with local scoundrel **Mr Willoughby**. Unfortunately, Willoughby is not only a scoundrel, but also tall and handsome, wears a many caped coat and is, basically, a sex god, so poor Marianne completely fails to realise that: 1) he's a bastard, or 2) her real hero is the rich, kind, quiet **Colonel Brandon**. Brandon, therefore, has to hang about for ages, waiting for Willoughby's true depravity to be revealed, before he can make his move. There are quite a lot of family complexities in the plot: Edward Ferrars' sister – a cast-iron bitch called **Fanny** – is married to Elinor's half-brother (a fool called **John Dashwood**) and it turns out that Colonel Brandon was once in love with a young woman, **Eliza Williams**, who was eventually married off to his brother, went mad with misery, and had an illegitimate daughter, also called **Eliza Williams**. She, in turn, has been 'ruined' (for which read shagged and abandoned) by Willoughby. Not content with this disgraceful behaviour, Willoughby then dumps Marianne to marry an heiress, and Edward is revealed to be bound by an unwise teenage engagement to a dreadful girl called **Lucy Steele**. Confused? Things all look a bit desperate for a while, but then Lucy runs off with Edward's brother **Robert Ferrars**, allowing Edward to keep both his honour *and* Elinor. He asks her to marry him during a – you guessed it – walk in the countryside. Marianne, meanwhile, eventually recovers from her Willoughby obsession and realises Colonel Brandon is a gem. Austen does not relate exactly when or where this revelation occurs, but I'm willing to bet shrubbery was involved.

PERSUASION
Hero: *Captain Frederick Wentworth*
Heroine: *Anne Elliot*

This is a lovely, lovely novel, with characters at least as appealing as any of the others; but it's quieter and a little less arch in tone – Jane in sincere mode, perhaps. The action concerns Anne Elliot, who at twenty-seven is considered to be as old as the hills and sunk beyond recovery into spinsterdom. The reason for this, of course, is that she turned down the man she loved, naval officer Frederick Wentworth, eight years ago. She was persuaded to this terrible course of action (the 'persuasion' of the title) by a well-meaning but clearly misguided friend called **Lady Russell**, who thought Anne was too young, and Wentworth too poor and unconnected. Ever since this grave error of judgement, Anne has been confined to a life of silent desperation with her vain-as-a-peacock father, **Sir Walter Elliot**, her arrogant and insensitive sister,

Elizabeth Elliot, and Elizabeth's dodgy friend **Mrs Clay**. But as the novel opens, Sir Walter is being forced to let the family estate, and the renters are none other than one **Admiral Croft** and his wife, **Mrs Croft** – who is, *mirabile dictu*, the sister of Frederick Wentworth. He, by the by, has risen through the naval ranks, earnt a fortune in Napoleonic war booty, and become entirely eligible, as well as being just as sexy as ever in his naval uniform. It's all pretty terrible for Anne for quite a while – she thinks he hates her; she thinks he's engaged to an idiot neighbour, **Louisa Musgrove**, who falls off a wall at Lyme Regis (long story); she's pursued by her repugnant relative **William Elliot**; and she spends a lot of time cooling her cheeks in quiet groves (of shrubbery, no less) and trying to put a brave face on things. But in the end everything works out, thanks to Anne being brave and Wentworth being passionate: he writes her a wonderful note (the eighteenth-century equivalent of a love-text) and all is resolved on a walk – not in the countryside, for once, but along the gravel-walk in Bath. If you've read Austen's big three and stopped there, put down this book, and go and get that one.

NORTHANGER ABBEY

Hero: *Henry Tilney*
Heroine: *Catherine Morland*

A satirical soufflé of a novel. Great fun to read, especially if you like seeing Jane Austen taking the piss out of eighteenth-century gothic novels, the *Twilight*s of their day. Catherine Morland is a kind, sensible country girl, who is nonetheless obsessed with novels filled with ghostly monks and rattling chains. On holiday in Bath, she meets and falls in love with Henry Tilney, who is clever and funny and slightly takes the mickey out of her at first, but eventually falls for her too. Catherine, meanwhile, as well as loving Henry, develops a girl-crush on his lovely sister, **Eleanor Tilney**, which allows her to accept an invitation to the family's estate, the evocatively named Northanger Abbey. The trip proves a wake-up call: she realises that not every antique chest contains a member of the undead; that Henry's father, **General Tilney**, has not, despite her dearest wishes, murdered his wife; and that sometimes a laundry list is just a laundry list. Along with these revelations come two subplots involving a rather ghastly family called Thorpe. **Isabella Thorpe** is a flirt and a gold digger, who, in the course of the novel, manages to befriend Catherine as her dearest confidante; get engaged to Catherine's brother, **James Morland**; dump him for Henry's brother **Captain Tilney**; then try to use Catherine to get

James back again when Captain Tilney dumps *her*. Catherine (who has also had to fend off a proposal from Isabella's moron brother, **John Thorpe**) is then suddenly sent home in disgrace from Northanger Abbey because Henry's father discovers she's not the massive heiress he has believed her to be. Fortunately, Henry earns his hero cojones by defying his father, following Catherine, and *during a walk in the countryside* asking her to marry him. I think at this point, even before the official thirty chapters of this book begin, we can safely give this piece of advice: if you don't want to marry a man, do not take a single step out of doors in his company – especially down anything remotely resembling a country lane. That way, clearly, matrimony lies.

MANSFIELD PARK
Hero: *Edmund Bertram*
Heroine: *Fanny Price*

This is the quietest, least glamorous of Jane Austen's novels, and Fanny Price is Jane's quietest and least glamorous heroine. Occasionally, indeed, some people, in the innermost recesses of their hearts, might suspect that *Mansfield Park* is a bit, well, dull. But actually, Fanny is not dull. She might in fact be Jane's most acutely observed heroine: a perfect psychological study of what happens to a sensitive child when she's sent away from her family to live with distant relatives, who are kind to her but never fail to let her know that she's poorer than them, dependent on them, and obligated to them. No wonder poor old Fanny falls for her gentle cousin (yet another clergyman!) Edmund, who never makes her feel second best and genuinely cares about her. It's the classic story: she's loved him forever, and he has no idea. It seems quite likely this state of affairs will continue till Fanny is old and grey and no longer capable of even getting *out* to the shrubbery, but then **Mary Crawford** and her brother, **Henry Crawford**, enter the action, and things begin to pick up. Mary is pretty and witty and a flirt; Henry is her male equivalent. It's love triangles (or rather, one massive love pentagon) galore: Edmund is infatuated with Mary; his sister, **Maria Bertram** (who's engaged to a well-meaning clod called Rushworth), is in love with Henry; Henry ends up wanting to marry Fanny; and Fanny loves Edmund. Various crises occur – a play is put on (a scandalous event disapproved of by Fanny and Edmund); Fanny is sent home to her poor, chaotic immediate family; and Edmund seems on the brink of marrying Mary. But in amongst it all, Fanny begins to show her mettle. She refuses Henry Crawford's proposal; she grits her teeth against the domestic chaos of her worn-out mother and coarsely spoken father; she acts as a moral compass for Edmund, who is going through a period of hopelessness (even heroes are occasionally hopeless) as he slowly realises that Mary is in fact a total disaster. Then Henry reveals himself to be a complete bastard by running off with Maria (despite the fact that she's now married to poor old Rushworth); Fanny comes back to Mansfield Park; Mary is cast off; and – eventually – a light breaks upon Edmund, he realises he loves Fanny, and all ends happily ever after. And even though this revelation is aided by 'wandering about and sitting under trees with Fanny all the summer evenings', he manages to pop the question without the aid of a country lane, or a confession amongst the shrubbery. Go Edmund!

BE NICE

I

So, first things first. Let us consider our model, the Jane Austen heroine. Who is she? What does she look like? How does she behave? And how can we all be a lot more like her, and thus attract Mr Darcy (or his twenty-first-century doppelganger, at least) into our lives?

There are two essential parts to the Jane Austen heroine (and, of course, to all of us): the external and the internal. The crucial take-home message from Jane on the external is this: appearance is not the most important thing. Oh, the relief! I hear you cry. Closely followed by: oh, the surprise! But it's true. In radical opposition to virtually every tenet of our superficial, celebrity-makeover-be-thinner-get-fitter-look-younger world, as a Jane Austen heroine the way you look is not of prime significance. It is not the reason people like you; it is not the reason you like yourself; and it is not the reason Mr Darcy will fall desperately in love with you.

For Jane, it's what you're like on the inside that matters. I hate to say it, but Jane's heroines are genuinely nice people. Even when they're occasionally excruciatingly annoying (ahem, Emma Woodhouse, Marianne Dashwood, Fanny Price), you like them, because they're honest, kind and have a sense of humour.

I know. It sounds too boring – not to mention unfashionable and weird and just plain daggy – to be true. But if you are channelling Elizabeth Bennet (and, ergo, Mr Darcy) in your love life, it's crucial to engage with this concept.

You need to try to be nice: modest, generous, and thoughtful of others. And, equally as important, you need to work on becoming nicer. Don't just imagine that some lucky few are born paragons of virtue and the rest of us are stuck wherever we happen to fall on the universal scale of goodness. A Jane Austen heroine actively tries to better herself – and not because it looks cool or because people will notice or because gorgeous men will fall helpless in her wake as she tootles around in the meals-on-wheels mini-van. Being a nicer person is a universal good; you do it because you're a civilised woman in a (supposedly) civilised society.

And, in fact, it *will* actually cause gorgeous men to fall helpless in your wake. And thus, it really *will* help draw Mr Darcy into your orbit.

A word of warning, however. Before Mr Darcy arrives to be amazed by your altruistic endeavours, you may need to brace yourself for an unexpected and apparently contradictory truth: becoming a nicer person will not get you *more* men. As a Jane Austen heroine, this is something you're going to have to come to terms with.

Miss Mary Crawford, so overtly charming and flirtatious, is always going to get more men than Fanny Price, with her serious outlook and her penchant for intellectual discussion. Marianne, full of wild charm and drama, is always going to be more popular than her sister Elinor, with her sense of duty and self-control. Even Emma, with her fundamental kindness and wisdom (albeit hidden under a lot of nonsense), is not as popular as Jane Fairfax, with her blond beauty and (frankly, at times rather annoying) air of hidden tragedy.

But Jane's is a model based on quality, not quantity. And, as a Jane Austen heroine, you do not want the thousand Mr Eltons or Frank Churchills of the world, after all. You want the one and only Mr Knightley. Being nice won't get you *more* men, but it will get you a *better class* of man.

This is because being nice is actually a miraculous sorting technique for separating the wheat from the chaff, men-wise. Fuckwits and dickheads and bastards, surprise surprise, are not interested in girls who are intelligent, generous and kind. They are not interested in girls who will spend twenty minutes at a party talking to the daggiest person present so that they don't feel left out while everyone else plays Strip Twister. Fuckwits and dickheads and bastards are interested in the girl shimmying between the red and blue dots, waving her bra in the air. So as you become more generous (Emma), more morally upright (Fanny) and more graceful under pressure (Elinor), you may find yourself shedding a lot of pointless blokes. This can be wounding to the vanity, but you've got to let it happen: you've got to have the courage of your convictions. It might even come as a relief.

This is a fantastic technique for everyone, of course, but it's particularly excellent for women who find that they repeatedly attract 'the wrong sort of man'. If you are such a woman, rather than undergoing extensive psychotherapy, just try focusing on being nicer, and calmer, and more accomplished in a quiet way, with no reference to men. Read better books, listen to some classical music, join a community project – and wait for the sorting process to begin. No bastard can withstand the combined weight of *Barchester Towers*, Elgar's Cello Concerto, and the Big Brothers Big Sisters Program. He will simply vanish into the ether, and we can all breathe a sigh of relief.

Of course, you don't have to revolutionise your entire life all at once. Nor do you have to go overboard. None of Jane's heroines are paragons of virtue, thank God, and we wouldn't love them if they were. Emma is vain and lazy, and makes wildly inaccurate judgements about people. Elizabeth Bennet is overly frivolous and lets her temper get the better of her. Anne Elliot lets herself fall prey to melancholy and depression, and Fanny is a boring old stick in the mud. We are none of us perfect (and it's worth remembering that our heroes won't be either), and that's okay. The path of true love does not rely on perfection, or only saints and angels would ever get together. So, you know, if every now and then you do end up in the midst of the Twister pile, don't be too hard on yourself. As long as you're doing your best most of the time, that's what counts.

So next time you're at a party and there's a person hovering on the edge of your group, draw them in. Next time there's someone standing by the whiteboard who doesn't know anyone in the meeting, introduce yourself. Next time someone tells a terrible, terrible joke, laugh anyway – at least enough to cover the deafening silence. And trust that virtue will eventually have its rewards. Genuinely kind, generous girls are incredibly attractive, and any worthwhile man (note the adjective) will eventually stop, and look, and take action. I have a friend whose boyfriend first told her he loved her after she'd taken the trouble to talk to his shy mate at the pub about paintballing; and Darcy falls for Elizabeth when he realises that her moral strength and sense of social grace are far superior to his own. 'You taught me a lesson . . . You showed me how insufficient were all my pretensions to please a woman worthy of being pleased,' he tells her. And we all cheer wildly from the sidelines.

BE HUMOROUS
—
2
—

Humour is not something self-help books talk very much about. One suspects it's part of the old wives' tale which holds that men do not like funny women. This, of course, is total crap. And yet a woman living by *The Rules* or inhabiting the Mars and Venus universe is rarely directed to cultivate a wry smile or the ability to see the funny side of life.

This might be because quite large chunks of single life are, in fact, resolutely unfunny. Dating is bloody hard work; especially internet and speed dating and all forms of organised-meeting-of-random-men-with-the-intention-however-wildly-improbable-of-stumbling-across-someone-you-might-actually-like. If you can't laugh at online dating, in fact, you may as well just kill yourself now, because it's hell on wheels, and you need a sense of humour just to survive it, let alone to have even a modicum of success at it.

Jane Austen knows this. She was, after all, a single girl herself, and a single girl who had virtually none of the modern-day distractions — no massage therapists, no pedicures, no cocktail bars — that we can turn to in order to soften the blow of vain/thwarted/non-existent love. In fact, a lot of the circumstances of her life — the early death of her much-loved father; the hypochondria of her indestructible mother; having no money; being a spinster; suffering from a mysterious and debilitating illness just as she was finally becoming well-known for her writing — were distinctly unfunny. But Jane — and this is the crucial thing — resolutely refused to be unfunny about them. In her letters, again and again, you can see her reaching for the funny phrase, the comic image, the joke at the end of the paragraph. 'My mother made her entrée into the dressing room through crowds of admiring spectators yesterday afternoon,' she writes in a letter to her sister Cassandra in 1798, discussing one of Mrs Austen's frequent miraculous recoveries from illness, 'and we all drank tea together for the first time these five weeks. She has had a tolerable night, and bids fair for a continuance in the same brilliant course of action today. [The doctor] wants [her] to look yellow and to throw out a rash, but she will do neither.'

She does the same thing in her novels. All Jane's most beloved female characters manifestly possess what the personal ads coyly refer to as a GSOH. In fact, their SOH is not merely G, but E.[1] Emma Woodhouse is constantly amusing herself (and Mr Knightley) with wry asides; Elizabeth Bennet virtually has to have the thumbscrews applied in order to say anything serious; even Elinor Dashwood is capable of a funny little dig every now and then. These are the kind of girls who have a sparkle in their eye; they always seem as if, at any moment, they might turn and give you a little wink.[2]

This attitude doesn't come naturally to most of us, of course. For most of us, slightly more Mrs Bennet-style behaviour – weeping in drawing rooms and wailing on chaise longues and telling everybody in earshot every minute detail of our frustrations/disappointments/failures – is more our style when it comes to matters of the heart. Humour, on the other hand, helps us behave like adults. And it will, ergo, help us find and keep other adults – male, Mr Darcy-like adults – in our lives.

So this is what Jane asks of us: to act like grown-ups. To employ humour – not to mention dignity, decorum, discretion, and other adjectives beginning with 'd' – in our daily dealings with the world; all those quiet attributes that we

---

[1] Okay. If you are pretending you are far too busy and important and eternally popular to have ever so much as glanced at a personals ad, I'll indulge you. GSOH = Good Sense of Humour. E = Excellent.

[2] I had a friend at university, Cecilia, who was a winker par excellence. She was also a deeply lovely person, so her winks never felt cruel or snide, but conspiratorial and sexy – proven by the fact that despite being a normal girl looks-wise, she felled men in absolute droves.

often abandon because: 1) they're boring, 2) they garner us no attention, and 3) let's face it, they take a lot of effort that *nobody seems to notice.*

Added to which, of course, is the fundamental truth that men really do love funny women. This is crucial. There is nothing – *nothing*! – so appealing as someone who looks at the world and gets the joke. You don't have to be the female equivalent of the Marx brothers; just try to cultivate your ability to get amusement out of life. Everyone – including potential heroes – wants to be around happy people, because they spread joy and laughter and other good things. I have a friend who is particularly good at this: even when her marriage was breaking down, she always maintained a fundamentally positive outlook on life. Not a crazy, ignoring-reality febrility, but a kind of secret amusement at and enjoyment of little things: good coffee, a beautiful day, making a lovely roast dinner with crispy potatoes and Yorkshire pudding while a storm raged outside. As a consequence, everyone was always longing to be around her (and not only for the sake of supper), including – predictably – every single man who knew her.

At the end of *The Last of the Mohicans* – one of the great romantic movies of all time (although at times, surprise surprise, you need a sense of humour to see past the fringed-suede melodrama) – Daniel Day Lewis tells Madeline Stowe, 'Stay alive! No matter what occurs!' This is good advice, of course. But so too is 'Keep smiling! Regardless of what happens next!' Never, at the risk of losing everything, lose your sense of humour.

BE CLEVER

3

It is a terrible thing — even worse than crushing your thumb in the car door or having to pick up dog poo (surely two of the worst things that can befall you in the general course of daily life) — to pretend to be stupid to get a man to like you.

Of course, there are girls in existence who are far too strong-minded and confident to have ever done such a thing. They simply announce their Mensa membership to the world in loud, carrying voices and let the chips fall where they may. But everybody else has done it at some point, in some way, to some degree. Whether it's pretending not to understand the fundamentals of football (how many times has a sport-savvy girl sat, smiling through gritted teeth, while some man tries and fails to explain the high tackle rule?), or faking the fact that you can't change the light bulb, or back the trailer, or debate the future of democracy in a geopolitically fragmenting world, we've all, in our own way, pretended to know less than we do, in order to give a man the impression that he knows more. This, says Jane Austen, is categorically wrong.

You could argue, of course, that playing dumb is not actually our fault. From our earliest fairytale, we've all been inculcated with the idea that as women, our role is not to be clever. Beautiful? Yes. Sensitive? Yes. Trapped in a castle on a lonely hillside awaiting rescue by a knight in dazzling armour? Certainly. But clever? Not so much. No princess in a tower ever effects her own rescue by drawing up plans for a rope ladder, correcting for the effects of gravity on the arc of a pendulum swing, and sailing to safety over the dragon's head. Oh no. Instead, she sits around spinning or weaving or engaging in some diverting but essentially useless crafting activity until the knight finally appears. (He's been delayed because he's been preoccupied on the other side of the hill, waving his sword and spurring his charger and showing the dragon how big his lance is.)

Jane Austen's heroines *are* rescued by men – mostly from fates as spinsters, governesses or parental wranglers. But they never, never hide their intelligence in order to provoke such rescue. All of them operate, at all times, to their full mental capacities. Sometimes, it's true, they do let men get away with things. But they do so to preserve the dignity of someone they love, or because they don't want to betray a confidence, or because they don't want to disturb domestic harmony. They never do it to make themselves seem dumber than they are.

And nor, says Jane, should we. In its minor forms, of course, the pretence is harmless, and a certain amount of yielding and letting others feel clever is a necessary part of life. But it's a slippery slope, and in its more serious, elemental forms, playing dumb is self-destructive and dishonest, and can never lead to any good.

Yet we keep doing it – and more problematic still, we encourage other women to do it too. There is a famous phrase, in use everywhere today, that hammers it home, and it's amazing how often women say it to other women – even women they really love. 'The reason you're still single,' we say, 'is because you intimidate men.'

'You intimidate men.' 'You show them up.' 'You threaten their egos.' When the revolution comes, of course, anyone who has ever said such a thing will be first against the wall, the sisterhood be damned. And if you have ever said it – and let's face it, most of us have – stop right now and make a personal vow never, ever to say it again, no matter how good your intentions. It may be true; it may be just; it may be a profound acknowledgement of modern-day gender relations. But it makes women feel bad, and as if they're doing something wrong. And rather than looking for brighter, more confident, more well-adjusted blokes – rather than aiming *up* – it encourages women to dumb *down*, to make themselves fit a more mediocre mould. Jane would cry out against such a fate for any of her heroines.

Happily, the best way of guarding against this sort of thing is simple: just remember Jane herself. Remember that she came from a world in which women were presumed to be so intellectually inferior to men that they couldn't vote, or own property after marriage, or charge their husbands with domestic violence or rape, or even control their own income or wages. They were hardly ever educated; and if they were, they were taught to paint watercolours, play the pianoforte, dance, write letters and learn French – all usefully useless skills to prevent them ever dabbling in any area of world affairs that actually mattered (with the possible exception of an end-of-world hostage scenario in which an art-loving, minuet-performing Dr Evil only speaks French). Mathematics or science or law or medicine, of course, were absolutely beyond their feeble powers.

And yet Jane, a product of exactly this world (she received precisely this kind of education, though she had a kind and intelligent father – a teacher as well as a clergyman – who encouraged her writing and gave her access to his excellent library), became among the most intellectually sparkling, brilliantly clever writers in the canon of English literature. And in so doing, she created characters like Elizabeth Bennet, Emma Woodhouse and Elinor Dashwood as models for us all. When it comes to intelligence, these girls never take a backward step. On the contrary, Elizabeth spars with Mr Darcy; she tries to best him in argument; she treats him, horror of horrors, as an intellectual equal. Emma, too, regards Mr Knightley as an equal, and talks to him without reserve, telling him her thoughts and expecting to be taken seriously. And Elinor believes – rightly, as it turns out – in the intellectual kinship between her and Edward Ferrars, even when all belief seems hopeless.

And take note! Worthwhile men – Darcy, Knightley, Edward – love their heroines for their intellectual capacity. It may be startling and unsettling for these men when a woman suddenly reveals herself to have, you know, a brain, because it happens so rarely; but it's also stimulating, engaging, even titillating. Jane Austen's heroes love their heroines because of their ability to 'judge rightly, see clearly' in all things. Think of Darcy himself, finding Elizabeth's face 'rendered uncommonly intelligent by the beautiful expression of her dark eyes'. She's pretty, but she's also clever, and *that's* what captures his interest.

So we should remember this, and go forth unafraid. We don't have to make a point of how brilliant we are – which Jane would regard as distasteful and vulgar, anyhow. We don't have to rub it in. But we can, quietly, be just as brilliant as we like. And if a man is worth anything – certainly, if he's going to be a hero in our particular fairytale – he will rejoice in it.

BE BEAUTIFUL
—
4
—

As already noted, Jane is a great solace on the subject of physical beauty. In this age of obsession with the superficial and the external, she is both a comfort to the mind and a balm to the spirit, because she genuinely doesn't believe that you have to be beautiful to get the man. Not one of her heroines is exquisitely beautiful. Do you hear that? *Not one.* Take this information and grapple it to your soul with hoops of steel.

As it turns out, in fact, some of Jane's heroines are frankly pretty ordinary in the looks department. And not in an ugly-duckling-who-is-only-waiting-for-the-notice-of-the-hero-to-burst-forth-into-astonishing-swan-like-loveliness way, either, but in a real-life way that even true love can't transform. Girls like Fanny Price and Anne Elliot have irretrievably thin hair or small bosoms or less-than-perfect complexions. Even her best-looking heroines, like Elizabeth Bennet or Emma Woodhouse, are frankly described as less beautiful than other characters in the same novels. (Elizabeth compared to her sister Jane; Emma in contrast to Jane Fairfax. Indeed, Janes have rather a monopoly on feminine beauty – a little stroke of vanity we can, of course, forgive *our* Jane.) In Jane's world, the best-looking girl does not always get the man. Let's just have a moment of silent thanksgiving for that fact.

So what *is* Jane's view of beauty, and how do we apply it? Well, in this as in all things, Jane is a realist. She understands that though it's not essential, beauty – at least as much of it as we're capable of – does matter. It's important to look as nice and carefully groomed as we can, because it helps us put our best foot forward in society.

It is also a fact – and this is slightly less feel-good for us, but Jane would want us to face up to the truth – that men *do* like beautiful women. Even when it's a woman they already love, they like to see her looking beautiful more than they like to see her looking, well, not so beautiful. There's a great moment in *Persuasion* when Anne is at Lyme Regis, taking a bracing walk along the jetty. She's having one of those windswept, colour-blown-into-cheeks-and-eyes-sparkling-with-exercise moments that happen to women in novels (as opposed to real life, where we all just get purple in the face and sweat), and a passing stranger (who later turns out to be her awful relative

Mr William Elliot) gives her an admiring glance. Captain Wentworth (who has previously remarked, essentially, that Anne has gone so far downhill in the looks department that he scarcely recognises her) intercepts this glance, turns around to look at her, and has a kind of that-guy-thought-you-were-hot-and-by-God-you-*are*-looking-pretty-damn-cute-actually moment. Leaving aside the predictable element of male competition ('I might not be quite sure I want her, but nobody *else* gets to have her'), this is a big moment for everybody. Wentworth realises that he still has feelings for Anne – and Anne (who has been totally crushed by the earlier 'drastically downhill' judgement) realises she's still fanciable.

The other interesting point to note here is that being as beautiful as we can be is good for our morale. Just look how cheerful it makes Anne! Jane understood that there *is* a relationship between external and internal: between looks and feelings. Jane did not write *National Velvet*, the best pony book in the history of the world, but she would have understood the sentiment expressed in it:

> Velvet stuck the plaster on to the wide hard back. Mrs Brown glared at the star. 'Pray to God y'don't get fat, child,' she said.
> Velvet sat back on her heels aghast.
> 'You can't *be*,' said Mrs Brown, 'what you don't *look*.'

If you're trying to be a heroine, it helps if you feel you *look* the part. Mrs Brown and Jane Austen both know this.

So, what are the physical characteristics of Jane's heroines? What should we all be working on? Well, Jane's heroines have lovely skin – usually described by Jane using some variation of the word 'bloom'. They also have bright, expressive eyes. And – oh happy day – that's pretty much all that's ever said about their physical appearance. No hours in the gym, no detoxing or bootcamping or fun-running (hah!) required. Very occasionally someone will score a bonus point for 'regular features' or 'sweetness of address', but it's not the Paris catwalk, people. For our purposes, it's all about the low-hanging fruit.

JANE'S FIVE BASIC BEAUTY POINTS

1 BLOOM

Try really hard to get your skin sorted. If you have a naturally great complexion, give thanks on bended knee for it, protect it from the sun, and don't mess with it. If you have terrible skin, go to your GP and ask what can be done. Make a deal with yourself to spend $300 – the approximate price of any high-end pot of wish-upon-a-star-in-a-jar beauty product – on professional advice that might actually help.

2 BRIGHT EYES

I hate to say it, but dull red eyes are the result of two of life's great pleasures: booze and late nights. Cut them out, and watch things improve. But if that seems life-denying and counterproductive (how are you ever going to meet a man if you never go out and get drunk?), at least get some of those eye drops that constrict the blood vessels in your eyes and temporarily restore their sparkle. We must suffer to be beautiful, after all. But don't use them too often! Only on dates and when there seems a higher than usual chance of running into Mr Darcy.

3 HAIR (ON HEAD)

Get it cut regularly; if necessary, get rid of the grey; move hell and high water to find some combination of shampoo and conditioner that works for you. Above all, avoid frizz and/or grease, both death to hero heart-winning. That dry shampoo stuff? A miracle of the modern age. Use it. But remember to brush furiously after application, or you will leave the bathroom looking like Miss Havisham. If you earn over 100 grand a year, consider the twice – or thrice – weekly professional wash and blow-dry. We all know the mysterious difference between a professional job and anything we can achieve ourselves; and just think of the saving in time, electricity, and upper-arm energy.

4 HAIR (ELSEWHERE, BUT MOSTLY ON FACE)

Get rid of it. We live in the age of laser, Jolen bleach and, if worst comes to worst, tweezers, girls. Moustaches – do we have them? Yes. Do we need them? No. Ditto hair on chins, chests, tummies and even – unless you are French or have an indestructible sense of Gallic sangfroid – on legs and underarms. Your bikini line is nobody's business but yours. But it's worth having things at least under control enough that you can go to the beach without spending your entire time obsessively adjusting your swimsuit.

5 CLOTHING

Jane was very interested in fashion. She was always writing to her sister Cassandra about which muslin to buy, or making rude remarks about people's sense of style. 'She cuts her hair too short over her forehead, & does not wear her cap far enough upon her head,' she writes of one acquaintance, and of another '[she] was at once expensively and nakedly dressed'. Do your best with clothes, within the limitations of your budget and your life. Try to instigate a washing and ironing regime that allows you to keep some semblance of control over your sartorial world. As someone who regularly leaves the house wearing pyjamas cunningly disguised as casual day wear; and who also frequently teams tight black leggings with T-shirts, despite having a thigh-and-bottom region terrifyingly unlike that of Heidi Klum, I know how hard this is, but try.

What you're aiming for overall is the look of someone who cares about herself: someone with self-respect, who gets some enjoyment out of putting on the face to meet the faces that she meets. I once lived with two beautiful Scottish girls, Rhona and Marianne, and the interest, fun and sheer pleasure they got out of make-up, clothes and just dressing for work was an inspiration. Every day was like a mini version of a getting-ready-for-a-girls-night-out extravaganza. Without being the least bit obsessive or vain, they really cared about the way they looked, and that made other people care about it too.

And that's it, really: just trying to make the best of what we've got, in a completely non-Kim Kardashian surgeons-and-superboobs-and-hair-extensions-from-hell kind of way. And we should remember, *always*, that what's going on outside is far, far less important than what kind of person we are on the inside. I know this sounds like something out of *Sesame Street*, but it's important. Again and again, Austen's heroines triumph not because they have the biggest boobs or the lushest lips, but because they are kind, they are forbearing and thoughtful, and because they do not behave like spoilt, uncivilised children. In Austen's eyes, the greatest beauty in the world can never, never compensate for vulgarity, arrogance or vanity.

So take heart. As Jane Austen heroines, we will always be beautiful, whatever we look like.[3] Like the girl I met a while ago. She was obviously in the midst of some emotional crisis, and she was at that point where she was telling everybody about it, so she told me. She was a small girl, with beautiful Rapunzel hair, long and thick and golden, but otherwise just like the rest of us. Anyhow, she'd started going out with this bloke who she really, really liked. A couple of nights earlier, she'd gone to his house to cook him dinner – she took all the ingredients with her in an esky. They had a beautiful meal, a great night; then they went to bed and he didn't touch her. She asked him what was wrong, and he said (can you imagine?), 'I think I could love you, but I just don't find you sexually attractive.' And this girl, instead of bursting into tears or throwing herself out the window, got out of bed, stood stark naked in the centre of the room and said, 'But I'm beautiful!'

Then she put her knickers back on, picked up her esky, and left. And in that moment, Jane would have completely agreed. She really was beautiful.

---

[3] As Roald Dahl writes so brilliantly in *The Twits*: 'A person who has good thoughts cannot ever be ugly. You can have a wonky nose and a crooked mouth and a double chin and stick-out teeth, but if you have good thoughts they will shine out of your face like sunbeams and you will always look lovely.'

THE HERO

5

Well. What is there to say about Jane Austen's heroes? Except, of course, thank *God*. During those dark nights of the soul, when it seems impossible that any man will ever appear in our lives who possesses even a semblance of native wit, intelligence or reasonable dentistry, this little constellation of cravat-and-pantalooned men are beacons of hope: gentlemanly reminders that somewhere out there *are* men worth giving up our Colin Firth fantasies for.

So let us range, like Homer, among the panoply for a moment. If we were to gather Jane Austen's heroes together like the Greek gods before the walls of Troy, we would see Mr Darcy, of course, leading the charge: the alpha and omega of all things hero-related. But Mr Knightley is also totally gorgeous – more pragmatic and tough than Darcy, and far more outspoken. And for my money, Captain Frederick

Wentworth is also deeply lovely – a kind of sensitive action man. Slightly below these stars in the firmament are what I'd call, perhaps, the idiosyncratic or beta-heroes: Edmund Bertram, Edward Ferrars and Henry Tilney.

Jane is a connoisseur of heroes for the single girl. And the reason for this is that she herself is a single girl, so she knows exactly what we like. Tall, decisive men, who are successful (let's abandon political correctness for a moment and admit that lovely men are made even more lovely by having plenty of lovely money, not to mention sprawling Derbyshire estates or a fortune in maritime-war booty or an endless supply of orchard-grown baking apples) and intelligent and sexy.

Sexiness is important. For men who never reveal so much as a strongly moulded thigh or a nicely tanned forearm – Colin in clinging wet linen was a stroke of filmic genius, but Jane Austen would have rather set her hair on fire than actually write such a scene – her heroes ooze sex appeal. (It's no wonder the stage directions for the famous 1995 BBC adaptation of *Pride and Prejudice* were rumoured to include the suggestion that Colin Firth – the actor playing Mr Darcy – should imagine him with an 'almighty erection' when he sees Elizabeth after she's been out walking.) There are moments in Austen when you can't believe that characters aren't just flinging each other to the floor and shagging beneath the parlour table.

Jane's heroes' sexiness is important, because when it

comes time to look for an Austen hero in our own lives, it's good to remember that sex appeal does form part of the package. A lot of what follows might sound a little, well, dull – but bear in mind that it's all animated by this underlying, undeniable frisson. Heroes in Austen do not strut around showing off their biceps to the ladies (in fact, overt vanity is a very bad sign in a man, and Jane is totally scathing about the vainest man in her books, Sir Walter Elliot), but they possess something far more potent: unconscious, but undeniable, charisma. Austen would be the last person to ever deny us this in our own search for a hero. It's just that it's not the *only* thing you need. Remember, not only are you looking for someone to shag every night for the rest of your life, but someone you can talk to over the breakfast table every morning as well.

Apart from rampant sex appeal, then, what else have Jane's heroes got going on? Well, they are all clever. And (notwithstanding our previous discussion about heroines not dumbing themselves down) there's a crucial, albeit sexist, point to be made about this cleverness. Heroes don't have to be brain surgeons, but they must be equally clever, or a little cleverer, than their heroines. If both members of a couple are a bit eccentric (the Admiral and Mrs Croft in *Persuasion*, for example), or a bit slow (Harriet Smith and Robert Martin in *Emma* – though Martin actually seems a fair bit brighter than dozy Harriet), that's fine. What won't work is a situation where the heroine is cleverer than the hero, or vice versa. That's why (apart from general smarminess), Emma Woodhouse couldn't marry Mr Elton or Elizabeth Bennet Mr Collins, and why Fanny Price – far superior in moral intelligence – could have nothing to do with Henry Crawford. And conversely, it's why Elizabeth and Darcy, Emma and Knightley, Anne Elliot and Wentworth, and Elinor Dashwood and Edward seem so balanced and well-suited: they match intellectually.

Beyond pure intellect, Austen's heroes are reading men: men who are interested in ideas, and the world, and – an important characteristic of such men – other people and their opinions. And they are all interested in talking, too. Conversation and interaction, even for aloof Mr Darcy, forms an essential part of their lives. They are men of thought and words as well as action. The value of these qualities to their heroines is incalculable. If your boyfriend just generally likes talking, it's far more likely he will talk to you, and this is really, really important. Women who think they want the strong silent type or the man whose still waters run deep are kidding themselves. As a friend once said to me: 'You've got to be able to talk to your husband. Because in the end, all you've got left is conversation.' She's right. It's not sex that bonds you with someone; it's chat: telling each other your fears and dreams and secrets and hopes and the true depth of your hatred for Collingwood Football Club.

So, Jane Austen would suggest you look for someone who's clever – at least as clever as you – and someone who talks. She'd also suggest someone who already has female friends, or at least women in his life he's close to. Darcy and Wentworth are devoted to their sisters; Knightley is Emma's friend long before he's her lover; Edmund is Fanny's childhood companion as well as champion; and Edward is Elinor's apparently platonic friend and kindred spirit. 'I felt that I admired you,' he tells her remorsefully at the end of *Sense and Sensibility*, 'but I told myself it was only friendship . . . I did not know how far [in love] I had got.'

So. Clever, engaged, a talker at some level, and fond of women. Now come a little cluster of qualities that it's hard to separate; they are also the worthy, apparently unexciting ones, which makes it more of a temptation to lump them together. Jane Austen's heroes are kind, generous, modest, and willing to own their mistakes. These things may not sound romantic, but just wait until your boyfriend has come and picked you up in the cold or the pouring rain (as Knightley does for Miss Bates and her niece), or bought you a perfect necklace for your pendant even though you never mentioned it (as Edmund does for Fanny), or refused to garner public credit for saving your family's honour (gorgeous, gorgeous Darcy), or taken responsibility for his actions in stuffing things up (take a bow, both Wentworth and Darcy). *Then* tell me how unromantic such qualities seem.

As with heroines, humour has to be somewhere in the mix, too. Admittedly, sometimes it's hard to spot: Darcy seems not to tell a joke ever, and Edward and Edmund are scarcely better (though they do very gently rib their heroines from time to time). But we must infer a sense of humour in all these cases, both because Jane created these characters, and she herself was so funny and valued humour so highly; and because her heroes fall in love with funny women. As we know, Elizabeth and Emma are capable of a very good joke, and so is Anne. You've got to assume that the men who love them love their humour, too.

And finally, even Jane Austen's heroes aren't perfect. They have less than desirable qualities: Darcy's arrogance, Wentworth's pride, Edmund's prosiness. They have their bad moments: their spurts of temper, their angry conversations, their thoughtless acts. They sometimes get it wrong, or act out of self-interest, or – a great, great failing of men in every age since the dawn of time – completely fail to read the subtext of the situation. The Jane Austen heroine needs to remember this and take heart, when dealing with her hero. The path of true love, even with a man in long boots and a cravat, never did run smooth.

THE BASTARDS
6

In life as well as literature, men – both good and bad – can be cunningly camouflaged. Jane Austen knew this, which is why she spends a lot of time and energy not only developing her heroes, but polishing her bastards to a high sheen as well. And in so doing, she gives her heroines a set of techniques to help them – and us – spot such men, manoeuvre round them, and generally keep them from swinging their dastardly wrecking balls through our lives.

Let's acknowledge at the outset that it can be hard to remember there actually *are* bastards in Jane Austen. You might think such outliers didn't exist in the eighteenth or nineteenth centuries; that all of society was one perfectly ordered whole in which witty, nicely dressed, essentially respectable people met each other in lots of terrifically civilised ways, like assemblies and balls and country-house parties, and nobody ever behaved badly. In which case, of course, you would be wildly wrong. Jane lived in a world teeming with suspiciously stylish vicars and louche lupine lotharios and people travelling lengthily on the continent for their 'health' – she knew all about single men who were mad, bad, and dangerous to know.[4]

So don't be lulled into a false sense of confidence that there are no really nasty men in Austen. Don't let yourself think, for instance, anything along the lines of: 'Of course Wickham's a bit of a cad (but he has that twinkle in his eye!) . . . and Willoughby's misguided (but so sexy!) . . . and Henry Crawford is a bit frivolous (but so much fun!), but none of them are *really* terrible, are they?'

Yes they *are*! This is what bastards do – lull us with their deadly charm before they stab us with the rapier cunningly

---

[4] Think of Jane's direct contemporary Byron. He was rumoured to have fathered a child with his own half-sister Augusta Leigh, and drove another erstwhile lover, Lady Caroline Lamb, so completely demented that when he spurned her she sent him a letter containing *clippings of her own pubic hair*. Byron, in fact, seems to have been connected with most of the melodrama of the eighteenth century: he was also a witness to the second marriage of Jane Austen's own neighbour, the third Earl of Lymington, and rumoured to be one of Lymington's wife's lovers. Lord Lymington himself was one of Jane's father's former pupils, and he sounds extremely odd: he was obsessed with funerals and slaughterhouses; he beat his servants and animals (on one occasion he broke his coachman's leg); and he got (perhaps) his just desserts: he was whipped and tortured by his utterly vicious-sounding second wife. Jane may have lived in rural seclusion, but freaks and weirdos and people you really don't want to know exist everywhere – even in the English countryside.

hidden in their champagne-buffed boot. Let's just take a clear-eyed look at these three, for instance. All of them behave *appallingly* in relation to women. Even before *Pride and Prejudice* begins, Wickham has attempted to seduce and elope with Darcy's sister Georgiana, who is as a babe unborn in the innocence stakes, and still only in her teens; and towards the end of *Mansfield Park* Henry Crawford runs away with Maria Rushworth (nee Bertram, Edmund's sister), thus wrecking her marriage, her reputation, and pretty much her life forever. Willoughby, if possible, is even worse: he's not only run off with poor young Eliza Williams (the daughter of Colonel Brandon's dead sister-in-law) before *Sense and Sensibility* begins, he's *had sex with her, failed to marry her, got her pregnant and abandoned his child!* It's all very well carrying Marianne manfully down the hill and shouldering his way into the house smelling of cold air and leather. This looks good and means *nothing*! The brutal fact of the matter is he is a *complete and utter shit*!

We forget this at our peril. Willoughby, in fact – and Wickham and Crawford to a lesser degree – provide an important bastard lesson: horrible men can be wildly attractive. Many of us know this from painful personal experience. And this is a large part of what makes the bastard problematic. You meet a man, he's charm personified, and what is more, he is *sex on legs*. How can anything possibly be wrong?

In fact, this rhetorical question is your first hint that something might be. Wild physical attraction has many effects on the feminine mind (and the masculine one, for that matter), and the first thing Jane wants you to do when you find yourself panting with Marianne-Dashwood-esque desire is to get up from the chaise longue, limp to a mirror, look yourself squarely in the eye, and say, several times over if necessary: 'Beware! He may be a bastard.'

He may not be, of course – and you should certainly not give up hope that, indeed, he may prove not only to be the sexiest, but also the nicest man in the universe. But you should proceed with caution until you've got a few concrete details established. The tragic reality of life is that the man who seems too good to be true, alas, sometimes is.

JANE'S FIVE-POINT BASTARD WARNING SYSTEM
1 BEWARE THE MAN WITH THE UNKNOWN PAST

Without employing the services of a private detective or purchasing a sophisticated but easily installed bugging device over the internet, establishing a new man's background can be tricky. But tread warily around any potential hero about whom you know nothing. Ask questions about his background – not interrogatory questions ('Can you provide me with a police check confirming the absence of crimes against humanity? And three written references from JPs, ministers of religion or members of a respected charitable institution endorsing your basic human decency?'), but just little details you can *verify*. Look for inconsistencies in his stories: bastards often lie about small things as well as big ones. This is all pretty depressing and horrible, I know. But so is going out for three months with a lovely surgeon called Henry Jekyll and then finding a black Amex card in his wallet in the name of E. Hyde.

It's worth noting, incidentally, that it's not just Jane Austen who cared about people's backgrounds. Everyone in the late eighteenth and early nineteenth centuries was obsessed with antecedents – probably precisely due to the absence of reliable record keeping and decent electronic surveillance equipment. In Jane's day, if you hadn't been formally introduced to a man – i.e. if you didn't know exactly who he was, where he came from, who his family was and how much money he had – you were totally forbidden from striking up an acquaintance. You might see the eighteenth century equivalent of Ryan Gosling smiling at you as you crossed the village street one morning, but unless you'd been properly introduced by a mutual acquaintance who could vouch for him ('Mr Ryan Thomas Gosling is a Canadian, the only son of a travelling salesman and a high-school teacher. He has amassed a fortune of several million dollars through his efforts on the theatrical stage, and thus, despite his unaristocratic origins and his thespian bent, he is received in all polite society'), it was social death to acknowledge his existence – let alone fling him to the ground and rip off his shirt to see if those abs really *are* computer generated. The aim of this restriction, of course, was to protect single women – us – from bastards. Unsurprisingly – as we can see from the cases of Georgiana Darcy and Eliza, not to mention Lydia Bennet and Maria Bertram – success can never be assured.

The modern-day equivalent of the unknown man on the village street is, often, the internet date. Everything he tells you about his background comes with precisely zero corroborating evidence. So, as we'll see in the next chapter, although Jane is not against online dating, and in fact is in favour of it as a theoretical proposition, she's all about keeping your wits about you – and your checklist to hand – as you get to know anyone who emerges, as it were, out of thin air.

2 BEWARE THE MAN WHO TREATS OTHERS BADLY

Pretty straightforward. Good men – Knightley, Edmund, Edward, Darcy – are kind to others, behave honourably towards them, and (though perhaps not in Darcy's case, given his [deeply attractive, sigh] fundamental cynicism) believe the best of them. Bastards are essentially selfish, so they're unlikely to listen patiently to the Miss Bateses of the world, as Knightley does; or keep their promises, as Edward does towards the awful Lucy Steele. In fact, they do exactly the reverse: Mr Elliot, cousin of Anne Elliot, behaves atrociously to his friend Mr Smith, encouraging him into heedless extravagance and then abandoning him to his fate (and his widow to illness and penury) without a backward glance.

3 BEWARE THE MAN WHO MAKES YOU FEEL BAD

This is a subtler directive, but it's important. Even at Henry Crawford's most persuasive, Fanny always feels uneasy about him; he never makes her feel safe, happy and comfortable in the way Edmund does. This is crucial. A good man will never knowingly make you feel awkward or uncertain or ashamed. Sometimes you do feel these things in the Game of Love, it's true; but if a potential hero prompts them it's a Very Bad Sign. Think of Willoughby. Look how horrible he makes Marianne feel: ignoring her messages, cutting her in person and insulting her by letter. Such behaviour – even in the absence of other evidence, and regardless of whatever piss-weak excuses he later offers – reveals him, unequivocally, as a bastard.[5]

---

5 It's worth noting at this point that, by the same analysis, characters such as Mr Elton and Mr Collins, though excruciating to the last degree, are not bastards. They are stupid, foolish and smug, but they're essentially harmless. And we know this because although they make Emma and Elizabeth feel embarrassed, appalled, and as if they want to run screaming from the room, they do not make them feel bad in any profound sense. They're simply idiots – and the world, alas, is full of idiots.

4 BEWARE TRYING TO CHANGE A BASTARD

This is a cardinal rule when dealing with men of any persuasion, and even more true when dealing with bastards. The bastards in Jane's novels are utterly unrepentant. Look at Wickham, sloping off with Lydia, wrecking her reputation, and only agreeing to marry her when Darcy stumps up the cold, hard cash. Look at Willoughby, marrying a woman he neither respects nor likes for money, then scorning her in word and deed while wallowing in his own self-pity. These men don't change, and neither will any bastard you come across. Don't waste your time.

5 BEWARE FUCKWITTAGE OF ANY KIND

Let us be frank. Bastards are excellent at sophisticated manipulation and bad behaviour. They are particularly good, for instance, at what is technically known as the snatch-and-drop manoeuvre. This is the one where they start out wild with enthusiasm for a poor unsuspecting heroine, who thinks everything is going really well (though, interestingly, she never really feels secure – a fact she can usually only acknowledge with hindsight), but then at some point – usually just when she begins to think, 'This really could be developing *into* something', they come up with some *useless bastard* line like: 'Actually, just so you know, I'm seeing other people' or 'I'd just like to keep things casual' or, the old chestnut, 'It's not you, it's me. I'm just not ready for a full relationship.'

Ugh. Words fail Jane Austen at this kind of behaviour – but it is, alas, part of the stock in trade of bastards. And, as point 4 suggests, there is very little you can do about it. Jane, therefore, would simply advise her heroines in general terms: don't put up with no shit, girlfriend.

At the same time, don't be too hard on yourself. Most girls do get taken in by a bastard (or several) at some point in the long march of life and love, so don't beat yourself up if (when) it happens to you. Even Elizabeth, perhaps Jane's most intelligent – and certainly her most bolshie – heroine, falls under Wickham's spell for quite some time, to her own ultimate chagrin. Just try to make sure the fallout isn't fatal. As long as you haven't combined bank accounts or given him the keys to your Maserati, the aftermath will be mostly emotional, which is horrible, but at least you have the consolation of having learned a valuable life lesson. Once you've been branded by a bastard, you never forget the sting or the smell of burning flesh, and you're a lot more wary next time round. A sad loss of innocence, true, but as Jane would say, as innocence is lost, so does wisdom grow.

GO WHERE THE BOYS ARE

7

Once you've sorted out who you are (bright, funny and kind) and what you're looking for (a hero who is clever, sexy and also kind), the next step in your quest for Mr Darcy can begin: the step where, you know, you actually try to find him.

There is one great problem with romantic meetings, as Jane Austen knew only too well, and this is their element of serendipity or chance: the fact that even though you join the judo club, the rugby club and the 'we-guarantee-there-will-be-forty-five-single-men-in-this-room-every-Monday-night-between-6-and-8-p.m.' club, the way you *actually* meet a man is when you trip over his briefcase in the bus aisle on the way to work.

It's easy to get fed up about this. 'What is the point,' you ask yourself, 'of getting up at 5 a.m. three mornings a week to go to swim squad with the hope of meeting a lovely man (with broad shoulders and tapering hips) if I'm actually going to meet him when he comes to read the gas meter? Why can't I just stay home in my pyjamas and eat chocolate ice-cream in the meantime?'

This is a good question, as Jane herself acknowledges. Elinor Dashwood, Fanny Price and Emma Woodhouse all meet their heroes through family connections: Elinor's half-brother is married to Edward Ferrar's sister; Emma's sister is married to Mr Knightley's brother; and Fanny literally grows up with Edmund Bertram. None of them has to so much as stir beyond their own front doors in order to meet the men of their dreams.

On the other hand, Jane and Elizabeth Bennet, Anne Elliot and Catherine Morland all meet their husbands out on the singledom hustings. And this, I think, is Jane Austen's take-home message. In the absence of a family of gorgeous sons living literally next door (aka the Knightleys), or some serendipitous arrangement of the relations-by-marriage family tree (the Dashwoods and Bertrams), if you want to meet men, you have to go where they are. There is a one in a million chance that, indeed, your gas-meter reader really will turn out to be an erudite Adonis in khaki work shorts, but the fact remains that you are more likely – a million times more likely – to meet such a man while covered in touch-rugby mud or wearing an unflattering swimsuit. And you ignore this fact at your peril.

And so, says Jane, you must participate. As Woody Allen put it, some years after Jane, 'Ninety per cent of success is showing up.' Nobody in *Pride and Prejudice* necessarily *wants* to go to the ball at Meryton (well, maybe Lydia does), but everybody dutifully puts on their best embroidered muslins and piles into the carriage. And that's what you must do too. To have any chance of romance in your life, you've got to *turn up*. And not just once: again and again and again. You've got to put yourself in Fate's way: you've got to give serendipity a chance. It's exhausting, yes. But romance *is* exhausting. Get used to it.

Now, the next detail is what to turn up *to*. Lunch with your girlfriends, the launch of a new lipstick line or the annual Prada shoe sale do not count. You must *Go Where the Boys Are*.

All this, of course, was much easier in Jane's day. Eighteenth- and nineteenth-century romance began (if not at private parties or dinners) at organised events: balls, dances, concerts and assemblies. One attended these events with the express, albeit unspoken (unless you were Mrs Bennett, in which case you did say it, frequently and at high volume) purpose of meeting eligible men. Balls, indeed, were where all the boys were. Elizabeth and Jane both meet their heroes Darcy and Bingley at the same local ball – a rare double bullseye – and Catherine Morland meets Henry Tilney at the Lower Assembly Rooms in Bath.

This is all very well – so easy! So straightforward! So much beautiful plasterwork on the ceilings! – but balls are, alas, pretty thin on the ground for most of us these days: as are assemblies and routs and country-house parties. So what would Jane advise in a modern-day setting?

She would tell us to look for the modern equivalents of the Georgian–Regency ball. Social events at work. (Just keep away from the photocopier. Xeroxing your boobs at the office Christmas party always seems like a good idea at the time, but remember Jane. Dignity, girls, dignity!) Parties at clubs you belong to. (If you don't belong to any clubs, join some. Preferably ones that serve the double purpose of teaching you something you might like, and having a high quotient of men involved. Sailing clubs, hiking clubs, surf clubs, cycling clubs and running clubs are all excellent. Cooking courses are good-ish, though most men present will be either gay or using a voucher given to them by their girlfriends. Touch-rugby clubs are excellent, if touch rugby doesn't make you want to poke your eye out with a blunt stick.) Gatherings at friends' houses. These are fantastic, because they contain a similar quality-control mechanism to most eighteenth-century balls, which is that (almost) everyone present has been vouched for by somebody else. If you meet a man who's a friend of your friend, that gives you some vague reassurance that they're probably reasonably similar to you in educational/social/economic terms, and psychologically okay. This seems a rather calculating attitude, I know, but at least it gives you somewhere to start. And if nothing else, no-one you meet at your best friend's birthday is likely to be a flagrant axe murderer.

Speaking of axe murderers, of course, returns us neatly to internet dating – which also bears a passing resemblance to the Austen-era ball. (Mrs Bennett would have been online in a heartbeat, plugging in '£10,000 a year' without a second thought.) Online dating, just like Jane's balls, demands some sense of antecedents from participants (or at least a vaguely convincing background story), a formal means of introduction, and a first meeting (usually) in a well-lit public place. Of course, confidence tricksters and toad-eaters (not to mention axe murderers) occasionally infiltrate the electronic system, just as they did the Georgian ballroom. Even so, Jane Austen would have been in favour of the internet's judicious use. She would have advised caution, thought and careful investigation, but she wouldn't have rejected it as a tool in the service of happiness. She would have understood that spontaneous romance can spring from the most contrived of circumstances, and that anything that improves your chances is worth a shot. So, in her world, she has Jane Bennet pay a call on the horrible Bingley sisters in London in hopes that Bingley himself will be present; in our world, she'd be telling us to put some different terms in the search engine and trawl through the results again. Go on, she would say. Nerve yourself, and do it.

Beyond the internet, of course, there is *real life*. The most inspiring story I've heard of a modern woman actually going where the boys are is my friend Jo's friend, whom we'll call Louise. Louise, who was a high-powered corporate executive, got fed up with years of singledom, during which the only dates she had were with men who not only had God complexes and German-engineered cars, but also soft hands and ulcers. And so she became a mountaineer. One suspects there were a few stages in this process – surely she didn't just sling off her stilettos and set out for Everest – but by the end she was quite hardcore. She used to go off hiking in the Alps and sleep in tents with small explosive stoves and everything. And in return, lo, the men were everywhere. And not wimpy executive types, either; strong men with big rough hands, far-seeing eyes and hard muscular chests, all wearing that incredibly sexy mountaineering gear that consists of many layers and zippers and toggles, all of which looks fantastic on men, even though any woman wearing it immediately takes on the shape and dimensions of a bowling ball.

In this environment, Louise could take her pick. She became, according to Jo, an aficionado of mountain sex. There were blokes queuing up to pitch her tent and defrost snow so she could have a nice cup of tea (after which, one presumes, she could decide whether she might like to have a little lie down). She only gave the whole thing up out of sheer exhaustion – and also because, deep down, she wasn't all that keen on mountaineering.

And that's it, really: it's that simple. If you want to meet men, you simply have to go where they are. And, if at all possible, where other women are not. You must persist, and you must keep your wits about you and watch out for axe murderers. But once there, where the men are, you can give serendipity a chance.

THE FIRST MOVE
8

So. You've got yourself to the judo party or the speed-dating event or the pub on a Friday night. You are out, in amongst it, swimming in the full tide of (hopefully man-saturated) social life. Well done, you! But now what? How do you capitalise on this exemplary initial effort? How do you actually *engage* with the cute man beside the ATM machine in the corner of the bar, instead of just standing hopelessly by, wishing that: a) *he* would talk to *you*, or b) a masked gunman would suddenly appear and force the pair of you into the storeroom together, or c) you'd just canned the whole pub nightmare and stayed home and watched *Pride and Prejudice* on DVD instead?

There are lots of techniques that can help you make the crucial first contact with potential heroes, some of which (use of wingmen, conversational ploys, etc.) will be discussed in later chapters. But there are two factors we need to get firmly established at the outset.

First, the good news. When it comes to meeting men, Jane Austen does not believe in love at first sight. Occasionally someone – usually quite a foolish bloke – is much struck by a pretty girl on first seeing her (Jane and Bingley spring to mind), but more frequently – and successfully – couples in Austen fall in love after years of calm friendship (Emma and Mr Knightley, Fanny Price and Edmund), or from a position of neutrality, naturally increasing interest, or even, you know, active Darcy-esque loathing.

This should come as a great relief to all of us, because it takes the pressure off the whole infamous concept of the 'first meeting'. We don't have to worry about lightning striking or the *coup de foudre* or eyes meeting across crowded rooms or anyone astounding anyone else with the unearthly power of their beauty. Of course, one could argue that Willoughby and Marianne fell in love at first sight – what with all that rain and wet linen – but just look how *that* worked out. The important take-home message for us is that the Jane Austen heroine is not required to slay every man in every room she enters. Hurrah!

Now, the bad news. Jane Austen does not allow much in the way of proactive behaviour by women to meet men. She doesn't – at the risk of being condemned as a Lydia Bennet/Isabella Thorpe nightmare – allow you to ring boys up or ask them out or chase them round ballrooms or up the Bath High street. She is, almost entirely, a wait-for-the-man-to-make-the-first-move kind of girl. This can seem a bit limiting. But what you've got to remember is that Jane Austen forbids a lot of behaviour on the basis of it being undignified. We should take some comfort from this: she wants to prevent us from looking like total morons; or from being hideously and publicly rejected; or from losing every last skerrick of our self-respect and being unable to show our faces in public for the next several thousand years.

And it's also worth bearing in mind that she doesn't forbid everything.

WHAT JANE AUSTEN DOES ALLOW
1 YOU ARE ALLOWED TO GO TO THE LOO

The eighteenth-century equivalent of this was to 'take the air' when the ballroom got too 'close' – in other words, find an open window when you could feel the sweat running down the small of your back. In the modern-day version, of course, you're not necessarily looking for the loo at all. You're giving yourself an excuse to: a) check out the rest of the venue for potential men, b) let the rest of the venue check *you* out, in case a potential man feels like actually making an effort to speak to you, and c) get away from your girlfriends for a second.

Although it doesn't sound all that dramatic, c) is actually very important. It's extremely hard for a man to approach a girl when she's stationary, on the other side of some kind of no-man's-land stretch of open ground, and, most intimidating of all, surrounded by her coven of BFFs. I know this because a single male friend explained it to me very earnestly one night. He called it his 'Pelagic Fish' theory, as in 'You've got to get mobile, like a big pelagic fish.' Creatures like tuna and swordfish, it seems, never stop moving their entire lives, because if they do, the water stops flowing over their gills and they drown. (Who knew?) But once you're alone, and in motion, a man can just accidentally-on-purpose also be in motion, and walking in your direction, and say something like 'Are you looking for the bathroom too?' or 'God, it's hot in here!' and you're away.

2 YOU CAN POSITION YOURSELF BY THE PUNCH BOWL OR THE FOOD TABLE

This is a party variation of the well-known folk wisdom that the way to a man's heart is through his stomach. If you spend half an hour by the booze esky or the chip bowl at any venue at any place at any time, it is a mathematical certainty that you will see every man present. And, also, if you're pouring yourself another drink or scraping out the guacamole, it gives you the same element of motion and activity that walking does, and helps promote conversation. You've just got to be careful that your proximity to the alcohol doesn't lead to your accidentally getting too drunk to stand upright.

3 YOU CAN TALK TO SOMEONE YOU KNOW WHO'S TALKING TO SOMEONE YOU LIKE THE LOOK OF

This possibility is beautiful in its simplicity. It's also the modern-day version of the eighteenth century 'formal introduction' requirement. If one of your friends is already talking to someone who looks nice, your worries are over. You have every reason, every justification, every green light in the world to just mosey on over and join the chat.[6]

4 YOU CAN MAKE EYE CONTACT AND SMILE

This is the most powerful weapon in your first-move arsenal. It is also, like a hand grenade, unexpectedly tricky to deploy, requiring a surprising amount of attention and hand-eye co-ordination. In theory it's simple. You see a man you like. You watch him until he, having the sense that someone is staring at him, looks over at you. Whereupon *you meet his gaze and smile before looking away.*

I have a friend, Leigh, who is fantastically good at this, and she has endless blokes keen on her. Of course, she also has many sophisticated additions to the basic smile – the

---

[6] Unless, of course, your mate fancies the person herself. Then you must, in the name of everything holy, keep away, away, away! For further information, see chapter 11 on The Wingman.

eyelash flutter, the hair toss, and the head tilt – but these are all optional extras: all you really need is the smile. I remember her explaining the mechanics of the technique to me one night at a surf-club party (potentially a very good hunting ground for single women, by the way: filled with wedge-shaped men, all six foot four). 'You've got to pick a bloke,' she said, 'and look at him. Then, when he looks at you, you look away. Do that a couple of times, then smile at him. Then wait for him to come over.'

'And what about the hair toss?' I asked.

'Yeah, you can do that, but you don't have to. If you do it, it's probably best just as you're sort of looking away.' Lee demonstrated, and I remember we both started laughing – the whole thing looked so much like Farrah Fawcett in *Charlie's Angels*. Needless to say, by the end of the night Leigh had the phone numbers of about half a dozen men, all drawn like lambs to the slaughter by her one-two punch of eye-meet/hair toss. (For what it's worth, I failed completely, but this was due to my inexplicable inability to meet anyone's eye, not a flaw in the theory. That's why I say, with the bitter knowledge of experience, that it's hard to deploy.)

If you don't feel comfortable with all the baroque additions, however, just stick to the basic eye-meet. This is mostly what Jane Austen's heroines do, with excellent results. Just think of Mr Darcy: 'I have been meditating on the very great pleasure which a pair of fine eyes in the face of a pretty woman can bestow,' he says of Elizabeth Bennet, and we know the great Game of Love has begun.

And if you can't even manage the smile, and just end up looking away in confusion/uncertainty/excruciating embarrassment, take heart: that may well be enough. Take a friend of mine, Maria. She was driving in her car one day when she thought she saw a friend in the car ahead. She drove up alongside him at the next traffic light, met the driver's eye, and was just about to smile... when she realised it wasn't her friend at all, but a complete stranger. Horrified, she looked away. But when she took off from the light, the stranger followed her. She changed lanes, and he did too – eventually cutting across three lines of traffic to keep her in sight. Totally freaked out, she turned off onto a side street. He did too. Then he got out of his car and started walking towards her. At this point, I might have slammed my door locks down and called the police, but Maria, who is Italian, is made of sterner stuff. She wound her window down and shouted at him. 'What the fuck are you doing? Are you some kind of maniac?' After about thirty seconds of solid screaming, when she stopped to draw breath, the bloke – whose name was Giovanni (yes, also Italian) – said calmly, 'When you've stopped yelling, are you going to come out for a drink with me?' That was eight years ago, and Giovanni and Maria have been married for five years.

STAND STILL AND SMILE
9

Just as getting a man to approach you can seem like a huge task, talking to a man you like can be almost impossibly difficult. Many of Jane's heroines – poor mouse-like Fanny Price and demoralised Anne Elliot, to name but two – are utterly silenced by the appearance of their heroes (just think of poor Anne, unable to even *look* at Frederick Wentworth when they meet again after the dire eight-year estrangement). This is because when we are actually face to face with, and trying to talk to, a man we fancy, we are often overwhelmed by a sort of meta-narrative that plays in our heads over the top of the real-life conversation.

This is how the meta-narrative goes, in the eighteenth century or the twenty-first.

You (or Anne Elliot), responding to Fanciable Man (or Captain Wentworth): Hello.

Meta-narrative: *Oh my God, he's here and I'm here and we're actually talking what's going on with my hair is my stomach pulled in what's he saying what did I just say what is my name who am I?*

Him: How are you?

You: Very well, thanks.

Meta-narrative: *Fuck!* (or eighteenth-century equivalent.) *That was so boring who says very well thanks why didn't I tell him about that funny thing that happened this morning when I broke the heel off my shoe would he like to hear that or would he think it's frivolous to wear high heels or has the moment passed maybe I could say it now but is it funny enough maybe he won't laugh maybe he will think I'm a total idiot what am I even doing here I'm sure he doesn't like me eject eject eject!*

There are three common conclusions to the meta-narrative conversation: 1) you talk for five minutes solid like a crazy woman in a strangely high-pitched voice and he thinks you're a hysterical maniac and never speaks to you again. 2) You make some pathetic excuse and leave the conversation in order to hyperventilate in the loo (Anne's strategy, though she usually goes to her room, or for a walk, or into the shrubbery) and he thinks you don't like him and pointedly ignores you for the rest of the evening. Or 3) you literally collapse from the strain and have to be rushed to hospital.

On reflection, 3) is probably the best outcome. Except that then he may think you're some kind of drug fiend, which is not great.

There is, however, a fourth way – Jane's way. It is, like everything about Jane, elegantly and deceptively simple: only four words. Stand Still and Smile.

This, it will stun you to learn, is really all you have to do. I know. It seems impossibly basic. But it's true. Throughout the eighteenth and nineteenth centuries women got men all the way to the altar simply by standing still and smiling. And, occasionally, nodding. Then the 1960s intervened, and suddenly we women were expected by men – and, far more significantly, by ourselves – to have opinions, and to express them openly in general conversation. Enter the meta-narrative, and doom.

Fortunately for us, there is the Stand Still and Smile theory to save us. Just think of Elizabeth Bennet. It's when she actually shuts up for a minute, 'too much embarrassed to say a word', on her fateful walk with Darcy at the end of the novel, that he finally confesses his love. And it's when Emma Woodhouse is so affected that 'she could really say nothing' out in the shrubbery with Mr Knightley that he's able to begin his own confession. Indeed, Knightley actually has to rally Emma to speech: '"You are silent," he cried, with great animation; "absolutely silent!"' That's right: and it's with silence that Emma, the great talker, finally gets her man.

The theory behind the theory, as it were, is not complex. Standing still is good because it ensures that you do not startle Fanciable Man. It's like hunting: you don't want any sudden movement to scare the wild animal back into the forest. To Jane, who lived in a world where men still regularly went out and shot things for sport, this would have been so self-evident as to need no explanation. And smiling makes sense because it's so encouraging. If someone is trying to figure out if you like them, if you're a nice person, or if you are their one true soulmate under heaven, seeing you standing there smiling and looking genuinely encouraging must surely be a good thing. It's also really important in retrospect: Fanciable Man will carry your smiles and laughter away with him after your encounter, and feel positive about you as a result.

So here's how you do it. You see Fanciable Man, you say hello, the meta-narrative begins in your head. This is your cue to just keep breathing, breathing, smiling, smiling, standing, standing, and let him do the conversational work. Eventually, you will calm down enough to get out a sentence or two, or ask a question. Questions are good – excellent, in fact. Men (and women, though men rarely realise this) love to be asked questions. And laugh as much as you can, too:

there is nothing so reassuring, so energising to the ego, as making someone laugh. A laugh is worth a thousand words.

What all this does is a) keep you interacting when you might otherwise run for the hills, b) provide Fanciable Man with a positive signal that you like the look of him, and c) give Fanciable Man the chance to take things further. Your aim is to let Fanciable Man have the last word — just in case that word might be included in a sentence like, 'We should catch up some time' or 'Would you like to go to the movies?' or 'You're the love of my life and I and my high-powered team of professional gift-givers would like to place ourselves at your permanent disposal.'

I first witnessed the power of the Stand Still and Smile theory one night in the pub with my best friend, Martine. In the course of the night, we became trapped by an out-of-work actor who'd just finished a stint on a terrible doctor drama, and who seemed, as a result, to be labouring under the delusion that he was, in fact, a doctor. He ranted on and on while Martine — who really *is* a doctor; you know, in *life*! — kindly nodded, and I stood there like a lump. Neither of us had ever seen the program, and since the program seemed to be his sole topic of conversation, there wasn't much either of us could say.

Oddly, this didn't seem to bother actor-boy, who just steamrolled on with his monologue, throwing his head back so his square jaw caught the light, laughing at his own jokes.

After about ten minutes, I realised he was actually really enjoying himself, despite the total absence of what most regular people would think of as conversation: i.e. at least two people interacting via the spoken word.

I didn't like actor-boy, so there was no meta-narrative to contend with (apart from an occasional, wondering internal remark along the lines of '*God*, this guy is a *total* dickhead!'), and so I was able to calmly assess the situation and realise how effective just standing there smiling and nodding actually was. An effectiveness proved by the fact that at the end of the night, actor-boy actually asked for my phone number.[7] (No doubt he would have asked for Martine's, what with their professional kinship and all, but her tolerance threshold for bullshit is far lower than mine, and she'd gone off to drink gin and tonics and get on with the rest of her life.)

So there you have it. One further point: if possible, it's worth implementing the Stand Still and Smile theory not only *during* conversations with Fanciable Men, but at the end of them, too. When you realise your chat is winding up, resist the powerful instinct to either a) launch into some extraordinarily amusing anecdote which will carry you

---

[7] I said yes, of course, because I have yet to think of a way out of giving people my number, and besides, there was the square jaw to consider. Of course, I was then punished for my superficiality and hopelessness by the fact that he never called.

seamlessly over the end of the interaction, or b) immediately invoke your busy life and lack of time by saying something along the lines of, 'God, anyway, I must go, is that the time, wow, yeah, anyway, good bye' and rushing from the room as if the hounds of hell are at your heels.

Instead, when you feel a pause coming, or a change in atmosphere, or some kind of concluding paragraph, immediately employ the theory. Let the dead air work for you. Let him figure out a way to end the conversation, because that end might involve asking you out, or making a confession, or asking for your number, or even kissing you.

Sometimes, in fact, the theory even causes men to ask you out *when this was not their original intention*. On rare but verifiable occasions, a long silence can push them over the edge, *towards you*. And then afterwards, because men almost always believe what they say and do, being both less socially sophisticated and less socially manipulative than women, they walk away thinking to themselves, 'My God, I asked for her number. Didn't expect to do that. Maybe I like her. Do I like her? I must. Anyhow, give it a shot, she seems really nice. Friendly.' (Friendly comes into his head because you've done all that smiling. You can be a psychopathic serial killer, but if you smile, men will think you're friendly.)

Obviously, the Stand Still and Smile theory should only be employed if you actually *do* want to give a man your number or have him ask you out or confess undying love.

If you don't, you should, under all circumstances, keep talking. Talk talk talk like a wild thing till you get the chance to exit, then get that car/pub/nightclub door open, commando roll through it, and get the hell out of there.

FEMININE WILES

10

Sometimes you go to a party, and you actually meet a nice man. Stunning news indeed – but every now and then it does happen. And if it does, you might imagine that the immediate aftermath would involve a sense of universal rejoicing: that you'd be bathed in a rosy glow of possibility for days afterwards. Alas, however, this is usually not the case.

In fact, what often happens to the Jane Austen heroine is that she comes home from the party at which she's met the nice man, and spends the night lying awake worrying that she has given him either: 1) absolutely no encouragement at all, or 2) not enough encouragement to lead to anything. This leads inevitably to the gloomy conclusion that: 3) he will never call. Charlotte Lucas expresses this fear perfectly when she says to Elizabeth Bennet, 'It is sometimes a disadvantage to be so very guarded [about encouraging a man]. If a woman conceals her affection with the same skill from the object of it, she may lose the opportunity of fixing him.' This is Charlotte talking, of course, who ends up married to Mr *Collins*, so we should take what she says with a grain of salt. Still, Jane acknowledges that the fear exists.

For women who are not naturally flirtatious (i.e. most of Jane's heroines: there are few Lydia Bennets or Isabella Thorpes among us), this fear is a constant problem when dealing with men. Like Jane herself, we feel most comfortable working on a 'little bit of ivory' – i.e. with the subtle rather than the supersized gesture when it comes to chatting up blokes. Going Where the Boys Are; Smiling; Standing Still and Smiling: these are all low-key techniques, the aim of which is to prompt blokes into chatting *us* up. They're techniques of subtlety and suggestion; of finesse – and as we know, Jane is all about finesse. But sometimes finesse leaves you feeling worried; as if you haven't done *enough*; as if Fanciable Man won't actually *realise* that you do, indeed, fancy him. This is what keeps you awake worrying after the party. But fear not! Jane, as always, has a solution. In fact, she has four.

FOUR WAYS TO FIX A GENTLEMAN'S INTEREST

1 BE WHERE THE HERO IS

This is a kind of personalised adaptation of the general Go Where The Boys Are theory. There is absolutely no harm, and no shame, in just happening to be where Fanciable Man is one day. Catherine Morland is constantly at the pump rooms, just in case Henry Tilney turns up; Emma Woodhouse stalks the countryside, waiting for Mr Knightley to return from London; Jane Bennet, of course, makes her infamous call on the Bingley sisters in London. And let's not forget Elizabeth Bennet, that most independent and reluctant of heroines, who actually goes to Mr Darcy's *house* while on holiday with her aunt and uncle Gardiner. Of course, apparently she only does so because she's sure Darcy himself won't be there and she's, you know, interested in the architecture and the garden layout; but had Sigmund Freud been travelling with her towards that mighty erection, he might have raised an eyebrow at such justifications. Nevertheless, the important thing to note is that far from being weirdo/stalker behaviour, it's all considered totally legitimate because Elizabeth has a *cast-iron excuse*. This is the crucial point. *You must have a reason for being where Fanciable Man is.* It's no use 'just happening' to be at footy training or in the boy's locker room or at the horrible dive of a pub beloved by your hero (unless of course you're a physiotherapist, a sport-facility cleaning professional, or a hopeless drunk), because you'll be completely transparent and, ergo, end up looking like a total desperado. You've got to have an excuse for your presence that doesn't involve bumping into the hero. Interrogate yourself beforehand, and if your excuse doesn't even convince you, it's certainly not going to convince anyone else.

2 FLIRTING

Jane is not really a fan of flirting. This is just as well for most of us, who are frozen with blind terror at the thought. If you are *not* (frozen with blind terror, I mean), you are a rare and valuable genetic freak, and you should stop reading this book and go out to the nearest pub and chat up a sexy man immediately. Do it for the sisterhood.

It's worth noting, mind you, that Jane doesn't object to flirting because it's ineffective: quite the reverse. Most men in Austen are just as susceptible to the old fluttering-eyelash trick as anyone else. Jane's a realist about this – she knows that despite the occasional suggestion that men don't like women who make the first move, the brutal truth is that most men will fall weeping on the neck of any woman who wanders over, looks them up and down, and says, 'Wow, you are really *gorgeous*.' The Mary Crawfords and Isabella Thorpes of the world, in other words. Men have their own insecurities to battle: they know they're supposed to do the legwork in matters of romance, but it can be hard work for them too, and a woman who takes the effort out of the equation is an object of awe, not criticism.

What Jane *does* object to is Harriet Smith-style doe eyes or hair twirling or listening to every word the hero utters with your mouth open and your tongue hanging out. This, in Jane's view, is just another version of dumbing yourself down, which, as we know, is anathema to her. Nor is she interested in raillery: in feigned emotion (Isabella), or taking the piss (Mary). (I have some sympathy for Mary, who can be very funny – though her humour is often linked to cruelty, which Jane doesn't like either.) What you can do with Jane's full approval, however, is engage in *banter*. This *is* a kind of flirting, but flirting raised to a higher power through intelligence, interest and humour. Bantering is what Emma does with Knightley, and Elizabeth with Darcy. Consider the following exchange:

> 'Do not you feel a great inclination, Miss Bennet, to seize such an opportunity of dancing a reel?'
> She smiled, but made no answer. [Mr Darcy] repeated the question, with some surprise at her silence.
> 'Oh!' said she, 'I heard you before, but I could not immediately determine what to say in reply. You wanted me, I know, to say "Yes", that you might have the pleasure of despising my taste; but I always delight in overthrowing those kind of schemes, and cheating a

person of their premeditated contempt. I have, therefore, made up my mind to tell you, that I do not want to dance a reel at all – and now despise me if you dare.'
'Indeed I do not dare.'
Elizabeth, having rather expected to affront him, was amazed at his gallantry; but there was a mixture of sweetness and archness in her manner which made it difficult for her to affront anybody; and Darcy had never been so bewitched by any woman as he was by her.

How lovely and enlivening and pulse-quickening is this? Everyone involved feels excited, titillated and clever. And this should be your focus – not beating your hero down by besting him in argument (a common mistake of the intelligent but socially uncertain woman), but lifting you both up. Don't worry about being funnier or cleverer than he is: if you are, chances are he's not your hero after all, so best to discover it early on. You want an equal, remember: and one of the best ways to discover him is via stand-up, chat-up sparring.

3 BE GOOD IN A CRISIS

This is unexpected, I grant you. But life is full of trouble as the sparks fly upwards, and however he-man your hero is, he will be pleased to know that you can cope in a crisis. When Anne takes charge after idiot Louisa Musgrove falls off the wall, Wentworth totally loves it – indeed he says warmly that there is 'no one so proper, so capable as Anne!' So don't be afraid of being competent. Of course, it is also true that no hero minds if a heroine is a bit hopeless at some things – operating a backhoe and killing cockroaches are two skills no heroine ever needs to master – but if you give the basic impression of being able to, you know, generally manage the slings and arrows of outrageous fortune, this is a good thing.

4 DANCING

All Jane's heroines dance and enjoy it – as did Jane herself – and being an elegant dancer is an enviable distinction. Jane recognises, further, that dancing gives her heroines a chance to engage more closely with men, and even *touch* them – albeit through gloves – which would have been absolutely forbidden under other circumstances. What really matters about dancing, though, is that it shows a willingness to participate. As we've already discussed, Jane values participation very highly. There's no sitting around complaining you don't like the music at Jane Austen's metaphorical disco: you've got to just get out there and do the Time Warp. She was herself an animated, energetic person: her nephew James-Edward described her step as 'light and firm, and her whole appearance expressive of health and animation'. She recounts her own enjoyment of a boogie in a letter to her sister, Cassandra, in 1798: 'There were twenty Dances & I danced them all, & without any fatigue. – I was glad to find myself capable of dancing so much & with so much satisfaction as I did . . . I fancy I could just as well dance for a week together as for half an hour.' It's easy to think, with all the focus on decorum and dignity, that being a Jane Austen heroine involves being rather dreary, somehow; but this is not the case at all. Jane loved a cheerful girl; so do heroes.

So get out and enjoy yourself. And one final note: don't beat yourself up. Even if you completely fail to employ your feminine wiles in any way, in all likelihood it won't matter. Men are notoriously pig-headed about matters of the heart. They are perfectly capable of pursuing women without any encouragement *at all*. Just look around you – the world is filled with Mr Collinses and Mr Eltons and even Mr Crawfords, all busily pursuing women in the very teeth of a gale of indifference from the women themselves. You only need to get them interested enough to make contact, after all. So relax. And keep your phone handy.

THE WINGMAN

II

Out there on the singledom battleground, amidst the cut and thrust and flesh wounds of your average Friday night, it helps to have an ally beside you. Someone to staunch the blood, administer fluids and hail the taxi in the pouring rain at 3 a.m.; a Pancho to your Don Quixote, a Robin to your Batman. A wingman, in other words. Jane Austen is a great believe in wingmen. Although she has the odd solo crusader – Anne Elliot, Fanny Price – most of her heroines have a trusty sidekick to assist in the hand-to-hand fighting in the battle of love. Emma Woodhouse has Harriet Smith; Marianne Dashwood has Elinor (and vice versa); Elizabeth Bennet, of course, has Jane.

There are two sides to the wingman concept for Jane Austen. There is *having* the wingman, and *being* the wingman. This is important. We are all, of course, the heroines in our own stories, the Elizabeth Bennets of our own lives – a fact of self-absorption that's excusable on the grounds that it's probably necessary on some deep subliminal level to our fundamental psychic health. But when it comes to meeting men, Jane Austen asks us to take a step in maturity and generosity, and sometimes *be* the wingman. That is, stand cheerfully by while someone else takes the spotlight; support someone else's aims, claims and efforts; smooth the path of someone else's psychological drama. Elizabeth spends quite a bit of time giving Jane a metaphorical fireman's lift towards Mr Bingley; Marianne and Elinor act interchangeably as lead and supporting actress; even Emma expends a lot of energy (albeit for her own amusement as much as anything) promoting the (deeply dubious, as it turns out) claims of Mr Elton towards Harriet. If someone as vain and profoundly self-satisfied as Emma (sorry, Jane, but Warren Beatty has nothing on Emma Woodhouse) can step into the wingman's role, we can all do it from time to time.

Jane's feeling is that the wingman/heroine roles should be roughly equally divided among friends. In practice, this means that, between two friends, you have some nights devoted to you, some to your friend, and some for free-for-all, laissez-faire activity. If you're part of a bigger group, you can either split into pairs, or have multiple wingmen for one heroine: a wing squadron, if you like. And if you have single girlfriends and you yourself are partnered up, I'm afraid to say your role is as a wingman from here to eternity. Such is life. Look at Mrs Weston in *Emma*. She is a full-time wingman for Emma; but she has a husband – and, latterly, a baby – so this is part of the natural order of things. To each according to his need.

Having established your respective roles, there are a few rules you need to follow.

JANE'S FIVE FUNDAMENTAL DUTIES OF WINGMEN

1 KEEPING TRACK OF THE GEAR

Holding reticules, arranging shawls, straightening ribbons. Checking teeth for mysterious green bits after visiting the tabouli table! Too basic to need any further explanation.

2 ASSESSING THE FIELD

The heroine may have a particular hero-target in view even before the man-meeting mission (i.e. the party, the pub, the hot-air balloon adventure) begins, in which case the goal is clear. Otherwise, the wingman needs to take note of the assembled possibilities, and present them in order of preference to the heroine. The heroine then makes her decision about who to pursue. The wingman's role here is one of unqualified support. No saying 'Really? You want to try to meet *him*? But he looks like a fireplug!' or 'Wait. Didn't he just pick his nose?' The exception here is if the wingman actually knows something terrible about the chosen target – then she's got to announce it immediately. Only material information counts. 'Wait! He's the guy who took pictures on his phone of that girl who'd passed out with her head in the toilet bowl at the surf-club party last week' is material. 'He's the guy who threw up at the surf-club party last week' is not. Everyone throws up at the surf-club party; this is not news.

3 DOING ALL NECESSARY INTELLIGENCE GATHERING

This means finding out the target man's name, vital statistics (height, weight, age – and also instances of TTDTWITP[8]), and relationship status. Finding out these details carries a risk that people might think the wingman likes the target herself, as when Mr Knightley's brother thinks Emma means to encourage the repulsive Mr Elton on her own account. This is deeply embarrassing to Emma, but in her role as wingman, that's too bad. The wingman, basically, has to suck it up.

4 THE WINGMAN MAY HAVE TO HUMILIATE HERSELF ON THE HEROINE'S BEHALF

(See above.) As long as no fundamental rules of decency and self-respect are contravened, the same advice applies. You are not the heroine tonight. Suck it up.

---

8 Terrible Things Done To Women In The Past

5 THE WINGMAN NEVER COMPETES WITH THE HEROINE – *NEVER*

This rule cannot be overstated, and actually applies to all situations involving female friends. If your friend likes a man and *expresses this liking*[9] – even if he doesn't know she exists, or, knowing, doesn't care – you can never, *never* think about him yourself. Even if he's your great soulmate in life and he's desperately in love with you and you with him. If she met him first – or, in our wingman/heroine example, if she picked him out of the available targets – that's it. End of story. This rule, and its pretty much universal acceptance by women everywhere, is one of the reasons the female gender has never begun a world war, or shot each other with duelling pistols in the nacreous light of dawn.

These are the basic rules of the Jane Austen wingman. Once the target is engaged, the battle becomes a lot more fluid, and the heroine and wingman will work out their respective roles as events unfold. The heroine might well be employing the eye-meet/hair toss; the Stand Still and Smile theory; or Dancing; she might also be Going to the Loo or Standing by the Chip Bowl. Who knows? But as long as the wingman preserves a sense that her tasks are to run interference (which may, for instance, mean chatting to the target's own

---

9 This is the crucial detail. Until – but only until – an expression of interest is made, he's fair game. But once the claim is staked, the discussion is over.

wingman – a role that commonly falls to wingmen of both sexes); to boost the heroine's ego in the loos if required (during a long mission, i.e. a whole night at the pub, this is often necessary); to not let the heroine make a fool of herself;[10] and to never, never abandon the field while the heroine is still engaged, things should work out okay.

Of course, the wingman has one final duty, which is to know when to go home. It can be useful if there's a pre-arranged signal about this, but hopefully you and your heroine know each other well enough to understand what's required. Elizabeth, for instance, knows that in those crucial final visits between Jane and Bingley at Longbourn, she can't compromise Jane's dignity or make her look desperate by leaving the room (despite Mrs Bennet's example); but she *can* give the requisite protection-plus-psychological-space to let the lovers triumph. This is a beautiful example of the wingman in action.

And in return, the wingman's moment will come. Having secured her happiness – and her man – Jane turns around and wingmans Elizabeth right back.

---

10 It is a stark reality that the pressures brought on by the heroine's weighty responsibilities may lead to her getting, well, drunk. In which case, the wingman has to stay sober enough to prevent her from trying to pash the bar man, take her clothes off in public, or have her photo taken passed out in the toilet bowl.

THE PHONECALL
12

Once the Herculean task of actually meeting a man is accomplished, what then? What does Jane suggest when, via some mysterious Austen-esque miracle, a lovely bloke *has* taken your number, and is – theoretically at least – *going* to call?

Jane is assuming here, of course, that you actually like the bloke – i.e. that you are interested in seeing him again. If you don't like him, don't waste his time or yours. Jane has no patience with girls who let boys pursue them because there's nobody better on the scene, or, worse still, who actually go out with them on the principle that the stale half loaf is better than no bread at all. Look at her attitude towards Isabella Thorpe in *Northanger Abbey*, who keeps poor James Morland hanging around while she attempts to ensnare Captain Tilney. Jane regards this as a spineless strategy, based on vanity and, ultimately, fear, and she will have nothing to do with it. All her heroines give very short shrift to men they are not interested in: Elizabeth Bennet to Mr Collins, Emma Woodhouse to Mr Elton. Even Fanny Price attempts, with a surprising exertion of her feeble powers, to get Henry Crawford to leave her the hell alone.

Assuming, then, that you *do* like the man in question: how do you handle the period between when he takes your number to call you, and when he actually calls?[11] This is a difficult time in the Game of Love, and you've got to guts it out. But before we get into the nuts and bolts of it, a note on the whole phone number/means of contact thing.

Contact after the first meeting, it will not surprise you to learn, was all a whole lot easier in the eighteenth century than it is in the twenty-first. This is thanks, once again, to the nature of the meeting itself: under the auspices of a mutual acquaintance, usually at a private ball or country-house party, where everyone was interconnected. This acquaintance could, on request, supply your contact details to your potential hero. Problem solved. (They may not have been very well organised about everything circa 1795 – democracy and universal suffrage spring to mind – but they really knew what they were doing in this regard.) Here in the

---

11 Note: if the man in question has already asked you out – you know, in person – skip this chapter (you lucky duck) and go straight to chapter 14 on First Dates.

modern age, things are more complicated – though if the man in question has your last name, Facebook is always a possibility.[12] Hopefully, however, he's asked for your number right out and the whole thing has been very straightforward. But if, for whatever reason, you haven't given him your details with your own fair hand, make absolutely certain he has them. Try to keep yourself out of the exchange (it looks a little desperate to actually inscribe your number in eyebrow pencil on the back of his shirt, for instance); but if worst comes to worst, give him your business card or your name and number and say, 'I think they were having a door raffle earlier. Could you put my card in the box if you see it?' Then smile innocently and leave.

Okay. So, numbers have been given, and noises about calling have been made. Your task is now clear. And conveniently, it's a task that has not changed since the eighteenth century, so there are lots of direct examples for you to follow in Jane's novels. Your job now is to wait.

I know. Hideous. Anathema to every tenet of modern-day, follow-your-dream, engage-with-your-life, go-after-the-things-you-want pop psychology. The problem with pop psychology, however, is that it tells you what you want to

---

[12] It should be said here that Jane would not have been terribly keen on text- or Facebook-based relationships. If a boy isn't brave enough and keen enough to want to talk to you in real life, as it were, Jane has doubts about his suitability as an Austen hero. You're the best judge of whether this kind of communication is a cop-out or not.

hear (one reason for its popularity), not what is true. But Jane doesn't care how hard it is; she just wants you to know the reality. It's not that she's unsympathetic to your plight, but her view is there's no way round it. You just have to be still, and breathe deeply, and embroider that damn firescreen, until your potential hero sees fit to call you.

And so your wait begins. Jane doesn't really mind what you do during this wait: any combination of walking, reading, watercolour painting is fine. Embroidery and voluntary work – taking food baskets to the poor etc. – are also excellent diversions. Her main feeling is just that you should stay busy and not sit around working yourself into a frenzy of anxiety. Frenzies of anxiety, such as that displayed by Marianne Dashwood when Willoughby ignores her so cruelly in London, are undisciplined, embarrassing and – most of all – completely useless. You can also discuss things with your wingmen/relatives/very close friends. But you've got to ration this indulgence, because it's easy to get swept into an orgy of self-absorbed analysis – often in the presence of wine and/or ice-cream – in which you allow yourself to get completely carried away. As Mr Darcy puts it: 'A lady's imagination is very rapid; it jumps from admiration to love, from love to matrimony in a moment.'

Don't let this happen, says Jane Austen. It's bad for your self-esteem; it's bad for keeping a grip on reality; and it's also just plain undignified. And if he *doesn't* call, it's embarrassing for you and for your friends, who've all spent three successive Friday nights convincing you he will. If worst comes to worst, you want to be able to say, like Jane Bennet after Bingley fails to call on her in London: 'I have this comfort immediately, that it has not been more than an error of fancy on my side, and that it has done no harm to anyone but myself.' Here is a girl with her dignity – and more importantly, her self-respect – intact. Compare this to Marianne Dashwood, utterly publicly humiliated by Willoughby's rejection in London: 'Marianne, now looking dreadfully white, and unable to stand, sunk into her chair, and Elinor, expecting every moment to see her faint, tried to screen her from the observation, while reviving her with lavender water.' This is humiliating for everyone – most of all for Marianne.

Another reason not to let yourself get carried away is that it can trick you into believing you like someone far more than you actually do. The persuasive powers of conversation with our intimate friends cannot be underestimated. You start out by thinking, in your own heart of hearts, 'Oh, him, yes, he seemed nice, we'll see,' and end up feeling that he is the most amazing man who ever lived and you will have to commit ritual suicide with your father's samurai sword if there isn't a text message in the next 45 seconds.

In those moments when you feel like you might be spinning out of control during the waiting-for-the-call period, Jane would advise taking a reality check.

JANE'S THREE-POINT REALITY CHECK

1 ONE MEETING IS ONE MEETING

However great a time you had on your first meeting, whatever combination of charming/sexy/funny/kind/clever characteristics Lovely Man managed to display, it's still only one meeting. Even Jack the Ripper managed to be nice on a first meeting. Well, at least nice enough to get those girls down a dark alley.

2 WHAT YOU NEED TO SEE NOW IS FOLLOW-THROUGH

Follow-through is important in many areas of life, not only golf swings and romance. In this case, if Lovely Man can't get his act together to consolidate a good beginning, he is patently useless to you.

3 THE FOLLOW-THROUGH NEEDS TO REVEAL ADDED NICENESS

For your own reassurance and faith in the natural order of things, you now need Lovely Man to show he's interested enough to pursue the acquaintance; and you need him to be equally as nice, if not nicer, on second contact than he was on first. So do not, like Marianne, kiss goodbye to your faculty of critical thinking. You are still in the information-gathering phase: be alert about what happens next.

Until you have proof of 2) and 3) from Lovely Man, it behoves you to have no expectations, and make no judgements.

The final advantage of Jane's wait-for-him-to-call strategy is this: it removes all elements of uncertainty. You don't have to torture yourself wondering if you should call or if he's waiting for you to call or if somehow you're neglecting some part of the social contract and all this time he's been sitting around desperately wondering why *you* haven't called *him*. This is not a possibility in Jane's world, and nor should it be in yours. Take comfort in a) all the groundwork we've already discussed, and b) a universal law of the male species: *if he is interested, he will call.* Women want to add excuses and exceptions and addenda to this law, but for Jane – and for us – there are none. When all the song and dance is over, when all the votes are in, when all the window-dressing is stripped away, *if a man likes you, he will call.*

Ultimately, this makes things pretty simple. Because if he doesn't call, he doesn't like you (or doesn't want to pursue you, anyhow), and it's not happening, and that's that. Either way, you are off the hook. So take a deep breath, send a little prayer to the matchmaking gods, and get on with your life.

WHEN HE DOESN'T CALL

13

As Jane Austen knew, it is a really demoralising moment to realise that Lovely Man is not, in fact, going to call. Whether it's right at the beginning, and he doesn't ever make that first contact after you meet; or whether you've seen each other a few times and he just stops calling, it's equally bad, though in different ways. In the first case, you have the loss of your fantasy of how great you were going to be together to deal with; in the second, you have the sadness of realising that someone you really liked (well, enough to see him a few times, anyhow) didn't like you (well, not enough to keep seeing you, anyhow).

Let's take the two possibilities, one by one. (There is, of course, a third scenario: the end of a proper, full-blown relationship. But we'll discuss that later.)

1 THE MAN YOU'VE JUST MET

Don't spend too much time bewailing the loss of someone you've just met. Giving him, say, eight days to call – a day for every year Anne hung around – is probably a good round figure. A week, plus an extra grace day. This is, in fact, quite a long time; after eight days you are completely at liberty to assume that he has been run over by a truck, joined the French Foreign Legion, or gone back into protective custody, and move on with your life.

Hopefully, if you've managed to stay reasonably calm in the preceding days, this shouldn't be too difficult: if you haven't gone around beating your chest and tearing your hair to all your friends, the whole episode can just die a natural death and never be mentioned again. This is why dignity is so important. I know dignity seems like cold comfort when you were hoping for the love that transforms the world, but when you're actually in the situation, you'll be surprised how much it helps.

Of course, you are entitled to feel sad it didn't go anywhere. The loss of any opportunity in life is, rightfully, the subject of regret, but you've got to keep things in perspective. Jane would tell you not to waste energy wondering what happened or hating Lovely Man. 'We must not be so ready to fancy ourselves intentionally injured,' says Jane Bennet, font of all wisdom. 'We must not expect a lively young man to be always so guarded and circumspect. It is very often nothing but our own vanity that deceives us. Women fancy admiration means more than it does.'

This is true. Lovely Man might have been a flirt; he might have just been having a good time chatting you up. Neither of these things is illegal. Or he might have really liked you, then woken up on Sunday morning and thought, 'Shit. That's right. I'm deploying to Afghanistan on Wednesday. She was just so gorgeous I forgot.' You can't know what was going on, so there's no harm in assuming the best. This way you limit your bitterness and your wounded pride; as well as allowing for the possibility that he *was* in fact deploying to Afghanistan, and he's going to call you in six months time and invite you to a ceremony in which he's awarded the Victoria Cross. There are more things in heaven and earth, after all, than are dreamt of in any single-girl's philosophy. Life is long, and weird: don't forget that. And in the meantime, stay graceful, stay cheerful, and get back out there next Saturday night.

2 THE MAN YOU'VE BEEN SEEING FOR A LITTLE WHILE

Things get a bit more complicated when you've been sort of seeing someone, and *then* he stops calling. Again, you should take Jane Bennet, that model of grace and good breeding, as your guide. After Bingley exits stage left, apparently permanently, she doesn't sit around wailing and vowing vengeance; nor does she sink into a decline (though she is, of course, very disappointed). She does three things. First, she remains optimistic; second, she does what she can within the bounds of good behaviour to figure out what's going on; and third, she calls on all her moral and mental strength, and moves on with her life.

POINT 1: OPTIMISM

He may call at any moment. He might be having a busy time at work; he might feel he's been being too keen and want to slow things down a bit; he might have developed short-term amnesia and be desperately wondering what the really important thing he forgot to do on Tuesday was.

POINT 2: DISCOVERY

Try, if you can, to figure out what's going on at his end. This does involve some work on your part. It also involves the potentially humiliating scenario in which you are, slightly, showing your hand – i.e. phoning/texting/Facebooking him. Just try to keep everything very lighthearted. Stay calm and cheerful; avoid extravagant or outrageous gestures; and try to convince yourself that it doesn't matter so much what the outcome is.

You can also drop by somewhere you know he'll be (with a good excuse, such as those in chapter 10 on Feminine Wiles); or to casually invite him to some (hopefully ineffably cool) event you've got coming up. Whatever you do, bear in mind that what you're trying to accomplish is to give him a little encouragement if he needs it; a little reminder of how fabulous you are; and a little reassurance that you're interested. Then step back, and see what happens.

POINT 3: MOVING ON

The hope is, of course, that he responds with wild enthusiasm to whatever you do in Point 2. The alternative outcome is, horribly, that he doesn't respond, or that he responds in a lukewarm way, or in a way that appears to be enthusiastic but you get the strong sense he's not genuine. In which case, Jane has only one piece of advice for you: get out while the going's good.

Again, this is where dignity is important. A Jane Austen heroine never compromises her self-respect; and a true hero never asks her to. If you are feeling embarrassed, ashamed or ignored, these are signs that you're better off out of there. You don't have to lose the plot or behave like a crazy woman or – importantly – say anything like 'This is it! It's over between us! And I'm taking the car, the dog and the jewels!' Focus, like an army in the eighteenth century, on retreating in good order and minimising your casualties. You know in your heart when it's over: you don't have to scream it to the world.[13]

One further note. It sometimes happens that a man you've been sort of seeing (or even *really* seeing, in fact) will come out with the fateful line: 'I think we should take a break.' There have, presumably, been some instances in the history of the world where this phrase actually means he wants to take a break, rather than it being code for 'I want to break up with you, but I'm too cowardly to come out and say it.' (See chapter 6 on Bastards – in particular, point five about fuckwittage.) In either instance, being calm serves you best. If he really means it, you haven't stuffed things up for the future; if he's trying to get away, you are escaping (from someone who may well be a bastard) with your dignity intact.

You may need to be quite tough with yourself about this. It can actually be surprisingly easy to keep making excuses,

---

13 Also, in the unlikely event that your instincts are wrong, behaving calmly allows for the possibility that your hero may call you the following day and confess undying love. Not a good idea to cling to this outcome, perhaps, but you just never know. I have a friend who was convinced her boyfriend was going off her: they had planned a holiday to Paris and she was sure he was going to break up with her under the Eiffel Tower. But she's a pretty stalwart girl – and she loves Paris – so she stayed calm, got on the plane . . . and when they arrived in the City of Love he asked her to marry him. He'd just been freaking out about the right place/time/way to ask her. On which subject, let me give a word of advice to all aspiring heroes. Paris is always right. Anywhere, any time, for any reason at all.

to hang around hoping, or to let yourself be in denial. Don't be. Life is too short to chase after men who don't see and celebrate your heroine qualities. There's a fundamental truth here: *a hero has to like you back*. And he has to do so of his own volition, not because you've tricked him or put on an act or slipped him a magic potion you bought from a hag on some blasted heath at midnight. He has to think you're terrific, without you moving heaven and earth to persuade him. So if Mr Wickham seems strangely blind to your charms, forget him. Mr Darcy is still to come.

THE FIRST DATE

14

In Jane Austen's world, the date as we know it didn't really exist. Thanks to the violently enthusiastic chaperoning of unmarried women during every waking moment of their lives, they were barely allowed to be alone with a single man for an instant until they were suddenly mano a mano in the honeymoon suite. The mind, frankly, boggles.

Here in the not-so-new-millennium, we don't have to face up to this horror, for which we should be devoutly grateful. But to replace it, we have something else: First Date Horror. And just like the honeymoon suite, it's just you and the man, eyeball to eyeball, with nobody to hear you scream.

Not that you'd want anyone else there, really: the presence of a third party at a first date is, in almost every possible situation, a Very Bad Sign.[14] I know this first hand, because I once went on a date with a bloke who brought his mate along, and to this day, I have absolutely no idea what was going on. Was he there to protect the date from my voracious attentions? To signal that the whole thing was in fact not a date at all but some kind of platonic threesome? To signal his interest in an entirely *non*-platonic threesome? Who knows. But it was one of the weirdest 45-minute periods of my life.[15]

Anyhow, in your own situation, as a Jane Austen heroine, you're (hopefully) going to be on your own with your potential Mr Darcy. This is a *good* thing.

There are essentially two possibilities for the first date: the drink date, and the dinner date. The drink date is a much lower-level proposition. Jane's equivalent of this might be the man in the ballroom who fetches an iced punch for our heroine. The dinner-date man, meanwhile, is the guy asking her for the first two dances of the evening, plus the final waltz. The first is a man still feeling his way, tentative but interested. The second is a man determined, through either natural confidence or sheer force of will, to stake his all on a single throw. Both have their advantages.

---

14 Unless, of course, the date is with an A-list movie star or European royalty, and they need a bodyguard to prevent groupie-mobbing or the theft of your date-gift diamond tiara by international jewel thieves.

15 Yes, 45 minutes is an extremely short period – good breeding normally demands at least an hour for a first date, and even that's only just acceptable. But, you know, that's still 45 minutes of my life I'll never get back.

THE DRINK DATE

The drink date, clearly, is the less pressured of our two basic date situations. (There is a third, dreadful possibility: the Adventure Date; but since this doesn't usually happen till much further down the relationship path, let's draw a veil over it and pretend it doesn't exist. Jane would have been utterly horrified by the Adventure Date.) Both parties usually arrive at the drink date from work, so the potential problem of outfit-stress is removed, though you should give some thought to the transitional outfit.[16] The drink date eliminates the need to worry about hours of intense one-on-one conversation: the whole thing is really just a low-key, getting-to-know-you arrangement that – all being well – leads on to the dinner date.

This does not mean it's not worthwhile, or that a man doesn't really like you if he asks you for a drink date. On the contrary, it may well be that he *really* likes you, and

---

[16] The transitional outfit literally 'transitions' from the office to the evening out. The LBD is a perfect example. Of course, it doesn't need to be something you really have worn all day while battling the powers of corporate evil; it just has to be something that the bloke can imagine you *might* have worn. And men have notoriously fertile imaginations in this regard. Thigh-high hemlines, low-cut tops, bondage leather: these are all legitimate work wear options as far as men are concerned. ('Of course she could have been carrying that black whip around the office all day. She has to let her co-workers know she means business.') So is long hair, that you take out before you meet, or put into some kind of loose arrangement you can pull out before you get to the bar. For some reason, into which we probably don't want to delve too deeply, men really like women in work wear with long, untamed hair.

doesn't want to stuff it up by going too hard too early. Many Jane Austen heroes like to take their time and consider their moves carefully – not everyone is as impulsive as Mr Bingley. In fact, nobody is. Mr Darcy, Mr Knightley, Captain Wentworth: these are all drink-date men. Consider, consolidate, commit.

THE DINNER DATE

Just because it's high intensity doesn't mean the dinner date needs to be a terrifying proposition. Depending on your man, the dinner date may be his natural inclination. Enthusiasts, like Bingley, often begin with the dinner date. I have a friend, Jonesy, who, during a ski trip with our mutual good friend Macca some years ago, agreed to what they called 'The Chamonix Declaration': a set of rules about their dating lives. Point number three of the Declaration became known as the No More Coffees clause. This clause was formulated by Jonesy (a dinner-date man) to stop Macca (a drink-date guy) just going out for coffee and/or drinks with girls, which Jonesy regarded as 'piss-weak and inconclusive'. The full dinner commitment, he explained, is a necessary part of properly 'giving a chick a go'. If a girl's worth asking out, she's worth asking to dinner.

So, you may be dealing with a Jonesy (or a Macca influenced by a Jonesy) kind of guy – a modern-day Bingley, in other words – in which case there is no escaping dinner. But it's actually really lovely and flattering for you. Take it as a compliment, and don't freak out. Again, it often happens on a work night, so your office/transitional outfit is fine. Just be prepared to do a little more talking than on a drink date. Remember the value of the Stand Still and Smile theory – or in this case, Sit. Have some questions ready to go – questions are excellent. *One* drink as a warm up before you get there is totally legit. (I remember a brief halcyon period where I had access to a (sadly limited) supply of Möet piccolo bottles, and I used to drink one as I was getting ready for these sorts of events. I've never had such a successful dating period in my life.)

In both these date scenarios, the most important thing for any Jane Austen heroine is just to *stay calm*. Keep breathing, keep smiling. If you really like the guy, try to bear in mind that he has asked you here (provided you've been playing by Jane's basic rules – if *you've* asked *him*, you've gone totally off-task, but good for you!), so he *must* like you, and you can stop worrying about it. (And if *you've* asked *him* and he's agreed, the same applies.) If you're not quite sure how you feel about him, don't worry. Think of it as an information-gathering exercise for both of you – no strings attached, no expectations involved. Remember that Jane doesn't believe in love at first sight: you don't have to hear bluebirds singing or see a rosy glow bathing the air around him – you just have to think he's nice. And if you actively know you're not interested, what are you doing there? Give the poor guy a break: let him spend his money where there's some chance of a return.

A note on this concept of return. No Jane Austen heroine ever feels she owes a man anything. (Well, Elizabeth feels she owes Darcy after he salvages her entire family from the brink of social ruin, but that's a special case.) It is a hero's prerogative to ask a girl out, make a fuss of her, spend some money on her. And it is a heroine's equal prerogative to stand up at the end of the evening, thank him sincerely, and walk alone into the night (where she will stay in well-lit areas, of course, and immediately get a taxi safely home). Nobody owes anybody anything in this transaction. If you're worried about it, offer to go halves in the drinks and/or meal (lots of men seem to expect this anyway these days as a matter of course, so you should be prepared for it). But never, never feel you have to agree to another meeting, or kiss a man, or God forbid have sex with him simply because he's taken you on a date. Or even several dates. Heaven forfend.

One note on the date-that-you-don't-want-to-repeat. If, at the end of the night, the poor guy asks you out again, and you just want to run screaming from the room/bus stop/taxi stand at the very thought, *don't*, whatever you do, agree. Instead say this: 'That's really lovely of you. I'm totally flat out with work at the moment, but why don't *I* give *you* a call if things ease up a bit.' The stress is important here: *you* are calling *him*, not vice versa. And then, you know, you simply don't call. I know it sounds a bit brutal, but it allows everyone's dignity to remain intact, which is really important – and which potential heroes, just as much as heroines, appreciate. It's also worth noting that despite their sometimes-hopelessness in taking a hint, I have never once had a man call me in the (very) few cases I have deployed this line.

Moving on. Whatever the date, wherever the dinner, however casual or exclusive or low key or dramatic it is, the important thing is to really focus on your basic heroine characteristics. Be kind, be generous: try to be a nice person. As already mentioned, stay calm. If you feel yourself in danger of freaking out, take a leaf out of Anne Elliot's book: go to the loo and take ten deep breaths. Try to remember that for many men, social situations are harder than they are for women – especially the one-on-one confessional dinner-conversation mode – so it's likely he's really going out on a limb for you. It can be helpful to forget about how overwhelmed you're feeling and think about him for a while. It's entirely possible, after all, that he's freaking out just as much as you. Or even more. A friend of mine went on a date once (drink date) where the man suddenly burst into tears over his beer. Can you imagine? Apparently he'd had a terrible day at work, and he'd really wanted the date to go well, and he felt it wasn't going well, and it all just got too much for him. Your heart goes out to him, but you can't help thinking, 'Dude, Jane Austen is not into self-pity. Get it together, man.' A first date is no time for extremes of emotion from either party.

That being said, you should forgive him if he's nervous or awkward. Take an interest in the menu on a dinner date; if at all humanly possible compliment the food. Try to be gracious even if it's not going well. If it *is* going well, show you're enjoying yourself. Laugh. Don't dumb yourself down. Let yourself be funny – if he doesn't get your sense of humour now, with the love light in his eyes, he never will. Try to invoke a sense of yourself having a happy interesting life, and this being a happy interesting interlude in it.

And finally, do what all Jane's heroines always do, because they are constitutionally incapable of doing anything else. Be yourself.

SEX

15

Where do we begin? I know this may come as a stunning surprise if it's a while since you delved into eighteenth-century literature (the genuine version, rather than the modern-day historical romance version, where no-one ever seems to do anything other than harbour French émigrés from the Revolution and rip each other's hand-stitched underclothes off), but Jane Austen doesn't really deal with, ahem, sex. Nobody in Jane's novels EVER has sex; the word is never mentioned; the topic never raised; the entire sordid business is, on the face of things, left safely where it belongs: in the nether regions of large country houses, safely buried below petticoats and buttoned beneath pantaloons and barricaded behind forty layers of sprigged muslin.

And yet. Sex was everywhere in the eighteenth century, a far more licentious age than the ones that followed. Indeed, by the time of Queen Victoria – and in direct contradiction of the fact that Vicky clearly shagged Albert virtually non-stop from the wedding night onwards, and adored every second of it – even *armchairs* couldn't show that they possessed anything as titillating as, you know, legs. In Jane's day, however, there was Byron and Caroline Lamb (as already discussed); there was Nelson and Emma Hamilton; there was the Prince Regent (later George IV) and his Catholic wife, his Protestant wife and his multitude of mistresses; there were strip clubs and brothels (as there are in every age, granted) and provocative theatre. In Jane's own circle, meanwhile, there was sexy cousin Eliza, who captivated two of Jane's brothers, James and Henry: both proposed to her and she turned them both down, before eventually marrying Henry (Jane's favourite, and ten years Eliza's junior) in 1797. And, of course, the consequences of sex were everywhere: children of every shape and size, filling houses, demanding attention and pointing out by their very presence that people were indeed busily doing the eighteenth-century equivalent of the wild thing.

This is just the general stuff of life, of course: Jane accepts it as she accepts the weather. (In fact, her mentions of children are rather lovely. 'Pray give my love to [a little nephew] George,' she writes to Cassandra in 1801. 'Tell him I am very glad to hear he can skip so well already, & that I hope he will continue to send me word of his improvement in the art.') What is far rarer in daily life, what she's under no obligation to investigate, and yet what she returns to again and again, is *eroticism*: sexual curiosity and desire. Her novels are filled with erotic moments: Elizabeth Bennet running into Mr Darcy at Pemberley; Fanny Price receiving the gift of a necklace from Edmund Bertram; Captain Wentworth gently detaching a troublesome toddler from around Anne Elliot's neck. The fact of the matter is that Jane fancied the pants off the heroes she created: Mr Darcy, Mr Knightley and Wentworth, and probably Willoughby and Wickham, too. She could not have written them so seductively if she had not. She could not have created those sexually charged moments between heroes and heroines if she hadn't imagined them, just the way we might (entirely theoretically, of course) imagine Daniel Craig coming home from the office and slowly undoing his tie, gazing intensely into our eyes, while we (who have suddenly assumed mysteriously Angelina Jolie-like proportions) mix him a dirty martini.

Given her interest in sexual *desire*, then, is there anything we can assume, anything we can infer in the way of advice, from Jane Austen to us, about the endlessly tricky, messy, fascinating business of sex?

Well, first of all, nobody in Jane's novels is giving it away for free. Except Lydia Bennet, of course, who is just an incorrigible slapper, world without end, amen. But in general, our heroes work hard for their physical rewards. None of them gets so much as a kiss until they've pledged their worldly goods to the heroines of their choice, for instance. But this, surely, is merely Jane abiding by the conventions of the day: it seems unlikely she'd demand it of the modern hero (or heroine). Look at her attitude to dancing: she's totally in favour of it – of the opportunity to connect physically with another body that we find desirable. Catherine Morland loves dancing with Henry Tilney and hates it with blockhead John Thorpe; clearly the point of the exercise is to get close to someone who gives you a little frisson.

Secondly, it goes without saying that Jane would forbid, categorically, having sex with anyone you don't really, really fancy. Nor would she ever condone sex as a tool of manipulation, a way of discharging an obligation, or of seeking reassurance, approval, love or financial security. In her own life, Jane's aunt Philadelphia Austen had been forced by financial necessity to travel to India as a young girl and marry a much older man she did not love. The whole family understood that this was, in essence, the exchange of sex for money: Philadelphia bartered her 'personal attractions' in exchange for her husband's money. Jane deplored such a fate: 'Do you call it luck, for a Girl of Genius and Feeling to be sent in quest of a Husband to Bengal, to be married there to a Man whose Disposition she has no opportunity of judging till her Judgement is of no use to her?' she wrote in a story when she was sixteen. 'Do you call *that* fortunate?'

The whole transaction, clearly, involved a negation of self-respect and personal volition she found untenable. Sexual attraction, in Jane's book, was an unbidden, involuntary force, and surely she would have regarded sex in the same light: as a power to be reckoned with, not to be taken lightly or manufactured under false pretences.

All the sources suggest that in her general life, Jane herself was filled with animation, sparkle and enjoyment. Her brother Henry said of her that 'her eloquent blood spoke through her modest cheek' – a lovely image of a demure exterior concealing a riot of feeling within. And perhaps this is a good analogy for how we, as Jane Austen heroines, should think about sex: as something gorgeous and exciting, running like an electric current beneath the apparently smooth surface of life.

Extrapolating this into action, it means that if we are getting lots of thrilling sex in our lives, there's no need to hire a town crier to tell everyone about it. No need for offensive PDAs or dry-rooting or grinding on the dance floor. And none of this utterly hideous-sounding behaviour we hear about (can it really be true?) of girls giving boys blow jobs in the backs of nightclubs. No, no, no, no, NO. Sex in Jane Austen is about reciprocity, complicity and exclusivity. It's not about power – no Jane Austen hero ever physically dominates a woman – or submission or degradation. All Jane's erotic moments are ones of equality: when Darcy and

Elizabeth run into each other at Pemberley, for example, 'Their eyes instantly met, and *the cheeks of each* were overspread with the deepest blush.' [My emphasis.]

Another important point is that for Jane, sexual feeling flows *from* emotional attachment, not the other way round. None of her heroines use sex (appeal) to get their heroes to like them – though Isabella Thorpe and Mary Crawford do, to their ultimate doom. So we should probably only sleep with someone once we've established there's an emotional connection between us; that the man cares about us, likes us, or, at the very least, is pretty certain of our name.

Nor should we abandon all sense of rationality and thought, even in the grip of the kind of attraction that draws Mr Knightley out into the shrubbery to Emma Woodhouse; or Darcy back to the Bennet's drawing room at Longbourn yet again. Jane would have been a hardcore safe-sex advocate, without doubt. Nobody needs unexpected babies or hideous and humiliating diseases stuffing up their lives: she would have whipped that condom on without a qualm. And it goes without saying that any hero worthy of the name would have been right there helping her do it – or at least keeping his grumbling firmly to himself.

And finally, there seems no possible doubt that Jane would want us to enjoy sex. Approach it with care, and some sense of deliberation, and a feeling that you really do want to have sex with this particular person at this particular moment. But then relax and have a laugh. Do not, for heaven's sake, lose your sense of humour at this of all moments. Sex takes more humour to handle than just about anything else in life: you need all the jokes you can get. The whole thing, after all, is so essentially ridiculous. Fantastic, but ridiculous. Jane – with her finely honed eye for the foolish moments in life – would have seen this with total clarity.

All this, of course, is pure speculation. Who knows, really, how Jane truly felt about sex – who knows how *anyone* else really feels about it, if it comes to that? It is part of the unknown and unknowable mystery of other people. Jane was a product of her age; she was a lifelong spinster; she had no serious long-term suitors. It seems highly unlikely that she ever had sex with anyone at all. But what seems equally likely – or as likely as anything can be, when filtered through the inevitable distortions of fiction and time and other people – is that she would have loved the chance to try it.

GAY OR STRAIGHT

16

Rather like sex, Jane Austen doesn't really get into gay relationships: the rainbow flag, alas, was rarely unfurled at Steventon Rectory. In this, as in many things, she was a product of her time – none of the village cottages of her childhood contained couples called John and James, or Susie and Barb (more's the pity) – and thus she remained a stranger all her life to the value of really expert advice about throw cushions and houseplants, or how to team Doc Martens with a camisole top. But even so, she probably knew more about same-sex love than we realise. She certainly knew about the sustenance to be gained from platonic same-sex relationships – there's no doubt that her sister Cassandra, for example, provided a level of companionship and emotional support to Jane herself that remained unmatched by any man. Indeed, women in the eighteenth and early nineteenth centuries often lived as Jane and Cassandra did – in all female households, independent of men – without exciting any particular interest; and it seems likely that at least some of these households were based on, or grew into, relationships of romantic love. In the same way, don't tell me that every gathering of lavender-waistcoated young men in pursuit of cravats in Bond Street circa 1800 was entirely platonic.

In Jane's day, men, for once, had a much harder time of it than women did as far as gay love was concerned. Poor old Oscar Wilde (admittedly almost a century later, in what was a far more puritan age) was utterly vilified for his relationship with young Lord Alfred 'Bosie' Douglas (who, just quietly, sounds suspiciously like a spoilt little so-and-so). Homosexuality was officially illegal and publicly subject to social condemnation, despite the fact that many of the great institutions of the English establishment – the great public schools, the church, the army and the navy – seem to have been, well, at least slightly heaving hotbeds of the love that dared not speak its name.

And yet, in everyday eighteenth and early nineteenth century society, among ordinary intelligent people like Jane herself, one can't help but think there must have been plenty of gay people of both genders calmly going about their daily lives. Indeed, there are several characters in her novels who make you wonder – Mr Collins (with apologies to gay men everywhere) is as camp as a row of tents; and Charlotte Lucas, for that matter, seems so unfazed by him that one wonders if men in the mass leave her unmoved. Fathers often seem to swing both ways, at least in potentiality: Emma's dad, Mr Woodhouse, could easily be a lovely fusspot old queen, and Anne Elliot's father, Sir Walter, seems to know far more about facial skin tone and complexion than any heterosexual man has any right to. 'Admiral Baldwin [is] the most deplorable looking personage you can imagine,' he announces at one point. 'His face [is] the colour of mahogany, rough and rugged to the last degree, all lines and wrinkles, nine grey hairs of a side, and nothing but a dab of powder at top.' One feels absolutely sure that whatever the eighteenth-century equivalent of gay man exfoliation is, Mr Elliot is doing it.

So what does all this mean for Jane's view of homosexual and lesbian love? Basically, I think she would offer exactly the same advice to gay people as straight ones. Maintain your self-respect; keep your wits about you; go quietly amid the noise and haste. And remember, incidentally, what peace there may be in honesty. Jane, in general, is not much in favour of keeping dastardly secrets – she'd be in favour, one feels, of coming out – but then again, she understood the pragmatic benefits of keeping one's own counsel, and following one's own heart despite the urgings of often misguided or actively ignorant parents and mentors (think of

Anne Elliot, of Fanny Price, of Elizabeth Bennet, all choosing their own unconventional paths in love despite the best efforts of those around them).

If you are a woman, what would Jane say about making another woman fall in love with you? Exactly what she tells all her heroines. Be a nice person; maintain your sense of humour; make the most of what you've got. If you are filled with confidence and chutzpah, make the first move; if you're not, try to Stand Still and Smile and not run screaming for the hills. Don't buy into any torrid emotional drama; don't create it; and don't excuse it on the basis of hormones, feminine intuition and sensitivity. All women are prone to these things, as all women know, which means two women together have double the potential for it, which is twice as exhausting and confusing, especially in the opening moves of the Game of Love. Just remember: everybody needs to stay calm; and nobody needs to get a tattoo.

For men, a crucial lesson seems to be to remember that relationships, unlike single life, are not all about sex. Well, of course, sometimes they are – but probably not the long-term ones. The sad reality, as for all men the world over, is that once you fall in love, you almost invariably get a lot less sex – and that doesn't change whether you fall in love with a man or a woman. All my gay friends report that once they find someone to love, their wild days as total floozies are done. Unless they are in free and crazy (or terribly mature) committed-yet-open relationships, they look back on all those hours in saunas and clubs as to a lost golden age. Then they go home and feed their dear little designer dogs and crack open the French champagne (gay men remain the only couples I know who can afford French champagne once they begin to cohabit) and reflect that life is not so bad, really.

In terms of actually getting a bloke to fall in love with you when you yourself are a bloke – well, as for all of us, it behoves the gay man to keep an open mind, especially where physicality is concerned. Occasionally the body beautiful cult of many gay communities can lead you a long way in the wrong direction in pursuit of the perfect pair of pecs – something straight women can certainly relate to (and probably gay women too, if it comes to that). And as we've already discussed, Jane does not believe that physical beauty is the best indicator of relationship success. Try meeting men in places other than online or in the gym; don't feel obligated to shag anyone you don't want to; and for God's sake keep the condom on . . . and, for that matter, the costume off. A lovely gay friend once told me how he'd met a new man, and everything seemed to be going brilliantly until they started kissing on the couch. Suddenly the new man got up, left the room, and reappeared moments later dressed as – wait for it – a full Roman legionary. 'Including the strappy leather sandals and a plastic sword,' announced my friend. 'It was the sword that did it. It was like a costume from Toys 'R' Us.'

In other regards, I have few fears for gay men. They are, after all, society's consummate heroines: they will take to Jane's suggestions like ducks to water. Indeed, they've probably been doing everything she suggests for years. What a gay man doesn't know about winking and smiling and tossing his ponytail is, categorically, not worth knowing. They are examples to us all.

THE NEW RELATIONSHIP
17

Incredible as it may seem, sometimes everything works out. Sometimes you meet a man, and through whatever mysterious workings of fate and Jane and the universe[17] (not to mention all the deathless wisdom contained in this book), you end up with a boyfriend.

I know. From the singledom side of the fence – especially the long-term single side – the whole concept of actually having a boyfriend begins to seem a bit like space travel: you can imagine the puffy silver suit and the zero gravity, but the whole thing just seems entirely *impossible* – you can't

---

17 My friend Lenny once told me about a friend of hers who went to the top of a mountain to ask the universe to sort out the various problems in her life. She had everything written down on a piece of paper so she didn't forget, and when she got to the top she said to the universe: 'Please give me a job. That is interesting. And allows me to work only three days a week.' History does not relate what the universe said in reply, but whoever this girl is, I love her.

imagine ever actually *being* there; or, if you somehow did get there, surviving more than a nanosecond before you exploded into a trillion tiny pieces. You are not Richard Branson, after all.

But sometimes it happens anyway. Sometimes, despite every indication to the contrary, you meet someone, you fix his interest, he asks you on a first date, and a second date, then a whole series of dates, and somehow you end up with a boyfriend. Someone fun and warm and sexy whom you really like, and who seems to really like you. Someone who even calls you his girlfriend, no less. The whole thing seems like proof that God exists, that the universe is benevolent, that all things really do work together for good.

This is the Power Ballad Period in any new relationship – the period in which you feel you want to spend all day standing on the edge of a cliff overlooking the sea, the wind blowing your hair back and your silk ball gown floating behind you, belting out your incredulous joy to the world.

You should certainly do this. It's a great moment – thrilling and energising and wildly exciting – and you should make the most of it. Jane, who despite always needing to slightly take the piss, was often very good at taking pleasure in other people's happiness (when her brother Francis's son was born in 1809, she sent him a poem that began 'My dearest Frank, I wish you joy/ Of Mary's safety with a Boy,/ Whose birth has given little pain/ Compared with that of Mary Jane'), and she would want you to enjoy it to the full. But she would also want you to exercise a little discretion, a little restraint, a little thought for those around you. When her heroines finally end up with their heroes, they are clearly delighted – actually, they're incandescent with happiness – but they don't shout it from the rooftops. Elizabeth Bennet battles manfully to make a joke out of it, even with Jane. Anne Elliot is filled with joy, but also quiet gratefulness and relief. Emma Woodhouse is humbled and – for her – surprisingly calm and serene.

Acting with a little decorum, at least in public (there is of course no limit to how many victory air punches or Beyoncé booty-shaking dance moves you can pull in the privacy of your own home) allows your still-single friends to be happy for you (or at least to manfully control their wild jealously and pretend to be happy), and your hooked-up friends (who inevitably had a huge fight with their long-term boyfriends last night) to welcome you to the club of coupledom. But remember: no-one is ever as happy as someone in the first, honeymoon days of a relationship, and you don't want to rub anyone's nose in it. Your friends are happy for you – just don't ask too much of them. Don't subject them to countless hours of conversation in which you extol the wonders of the new man and how incandescent the sex is and how afterwards 'he just held me' and 'we talked all night'. Don't demand that they tell you, again, how great he is and how you're glowing with happiness and how they always knew you'd find someone. Don't drag every conversation around to your relationship in the first thirty seconds. 'That's really interesting what you say about the debt crisis in Europe. Because [new man] was just saying last night how he felt like he was in debt to the universe now that he'd met me.' This is perilously close to Mrs Elton in *Emma*, discussing her 'caro sposo' and his attentions – and you know how everyone feels about Mrs Elton.

The other thing Jane would want us to do in the early days of a relationship, surprise surprise, is to not freak out. I know we've covered this before (in fact, if Jane's entire lexicon of advice about life and relationships could be boiled down to three words, they would be 'Don't Freak Out'. Or possibly 'Always Stay Calm'), but it's good advice, and surprisingly relevant, even in the honeymoon period. It's natural to be tripping gaily along, awash with endorphins and the rosy glow of new love, and then to suddenly think, 'Oh my God! I don't think he likes me! I think he's going off me. Panic panic panic!' Such thoughts can be prompted by him not ringing exactly when he said he would, or seeming distant one evening, or otherwise revealing that he may have the occasional thought entering his frontal lobes that is not connected to your jaw-dropping new relationship.

It is your job to take no notice of such thoughts. Keep laughing, breathing and going to work and, if possible, try to invoke a patchwork piece of happiness (see chapter 19) to rebalance yourself. Certainly do *not* raise your neuroses with him. I know this seems counterintuitive: surely the point about healthy relationships is that you can tell the other person every thought, every worry, every single thing you're thinking about. This is *wrong*.

If need be, ask yourself these questions as a means of calming yourself. Is he happy to spend time with you? Is he talking about things in the future for both of you to do? Is he making efforts on your behalf? Most of all, is he generally interested in you and your thoughts and what's happening in your life? If so, stop worrying.

A few further points. Heroes who really love their heroines don't try to change them. As a heroine in a new relationship, you should feel like you can really be yourself, and that self will be celebrated by your hero. And though you might feel anxious some of the time, especially when you're apart, the majority of your time together you should feel good and happy and relaxed – continuous anxiety, not resolved by being together, is a bad sign. And finally, if you do get anxious, and if you do reveal this occasionally, that's okay. Heroes are braced for a bit of drama from their heroines. (Emphasis on 'a bit'; bear in mind that a male's tolerance for emotional upheaval is far, far lower than the equivalent female's.) Relationships, even new relationships, are far more robust than you think. Remember Edward Ferrars and Elinor Dashwood; remember Catherine Morland and Henry Tilney; remember Mr Darcy and Elizabeth; remember indeed, every one of Jane Austen's couples. Misunderstandings, mutual offences given and received, anguish, drama – you name it, they go through it, but it all works out okay in the end. So take heart. If it's going to last, you won't destroy it.

MAKING LOVE LAST
18

Even in the first, fledgling days of a relationship, you might be surprised to find the way your mind wanders. One minute you're sitting on the bus on the way to work, thinking blissfully '[New man] is so lovely lovely lovely,' and meditating on his many miraculous qualities ('It's so amazing that he manages to exist in the world with only two pairs of underpants!'), and the next you're suddenly clutching the bus seat in front of you, screaming internally, 'How can I make him love me *forever*?!'

Then, of course, because you are a Jane Austen heroine and we have discussed this, you immediately begin a deep-breathing exercise, peel your fingers off the graffitied upholstery, and resolve never to raise this subject with your hero. But be that as it may, the thought is there. And all of us, even at the beginning of relationships when it's entirely inappropriate, will think it. It's a girl thing. So let's consider the question. What *about* the long term? How, in the name of all that is holy in the heroine universe, does Jane suggest we make love last?

Jane, of course, is not the only author to have addressed this question. Two hundred years after *Pride and Prejudice*, a grotty hippyish author called Tom Robbins wrote a lovely book called *Still Life with Woodpecker*, in which he asks, literally: *'Who knows how to make love stay?* [His emphasis, not mine. For once.] Answer me that and I will tell you whether or not to kill yourself. [Thus proving that melodrama is not unique to the female mind, or the Georgian–Regency novel.] Answer me that and I will ease your mind about the beginning and the end of time. Answer me that and I will reveal to you the purpose of the moon.'

Jane – who is far more pragmatic than Robbins will ever be – is not interested in the purpose of the moon; nor ostensibly, in long-term coupledom: all her heroines are in the throes of brand-new, being-born-before-our-very-eyes relationships. But in fact, she does have the old guard – the long-relationship couples – in her novels, too. There's Mr and Mrs Bennet; Aunt and Uncle Gardiner; Emma's sister and Mr Knightley's brother, Isabella and John Knightley; Mr and Mrs Weston; Captain Wentworth's sister and brother-in-law, the Admiral and Mrs Croft. So it's interesting to ask the question: have any of these characters, according to Jane, learnt how to make love stay? And if so, what's their secret?

Well, some of them certainly have *not* learnt any such thing. Mr and Mrs Bennet are a signal lesson in what *not* to do (marry someone who does not match you intellectually, with whom you have absolutely nothing in common), and how not to behave (harass and berate him; scorn and ridicule her) long term. But others – the Westons, the Gardiners, the Knightleys, the Crofts – are certainly happy together. And their happiness, according to Jane, rests on three things.

Firstly, and perhaps most crucially, is what we might call the alliance of interests. Admiral and Mrs Croft have the navy and Captain Wentworth to hold them together – as well as a shared love of rather swashbuckling travel and exotic foreign climes. Mr and Mrs John Knightley, despite great differences in temperament and apparent suitability, are bonded by their mutual love and attachment to home life and their children. And the Gardiners have a happiness based on shared good humour and an unpretentious, comfortable life in London.[18] None of this sounds very thrilling,

---

18 Of course, there are other long-term couples in Austen: the ones we don't like. But casting such personal bias aside, we should acknowledge that several of them are, in fact, perfectly happy, too – and tellingly, they share the same relationship success stories as the ones we love. Elinor and Marianne Dashwood's half-brother John and his execrable wife Fanny live together in perfect mercenary harmony, obsessed with the maintenance of John's fortune and not giving a brass razoo to anyone else; and in *Emma*, Mr and Mrs Elton are as happy as pigs in mud, social clambering their way through life.

I grant you, but as Jane would say, wake up. It's not about thrills; it's about real life. And in real life, having lots of things – or at least a few crucial details – in common is good news.

Secondly, all of these couples respect each other – always a crucial ingredient for Jane in any relationship, whatever its longevity. And thirdly, they have a tolerance for each other's differences. John Knightley puts up with Isabella's constant fears for the health of the children, as she puts up with his antisocial moods and grumpy-man foot-stomping. Mrs Weston, meanwhile, 'like a sweet-tempered woman and a good wife' gracefully adapts to Mr Weston's view of the passage during the ball preparations at the Crown Inn. Happy couples, Jane realises, support each other, and operate in a spirit of mutual support. Or, as Tom Robbins has it, in slightly more hipster terms: 'Instead of vowing to honour and obey, maybe we should swear to aid and abet.'[19]

Jane herself, meanwhile, has one final point to make. Don't take love for granted. This is hard, I know: hard when the realities of your Mr Darcy's everyday presence – his dirty cravats, his morning breath, his trance-like fixation in

---

19 Actually, for an unredeemed hippy Tom has a lot of very cool stuff to say about love: 'We waste time looking for the perfect lover instead of creating the perfect love'; 'Prince Charming really is a toad'; and 'My love for you has no strings attached. I love you for free.' Jane would have agreed with all of this. Then she would have told Tom to get a haircut, for God's sake.

front of motor sports or bikini parades – begin to tarnish his dewy lacy-cuffed perfection. But keep the faith. If you have a fundamentally good man – a Mr Weston or an Admiral Croft – try to cherish the good things: revel in the happy moments, and remember the (shocking) reality that you are not perfect either. Cultivate your shared interests; respect his right to spend several hours a week working on his model train set, even though it makes you want to crush all his locomotives with your bare hands; and tolerate his foibles, as someone who has some foibles of her own. Who knows? You might even end up like my mum, who once told me as we stacked the dishwasher one night that each day when my father came home, she still felt glad when she heard his car pull up outside. Not bad after forty-three years.

THE PATCHWORK OF HAPPINESS
19

It can sometimes be lost in the Sturm und Drang of the singledom rollercoaster, or obscured by the dense flocks of bluebirds of happiness that surround new love, but life is, in fact, not all about boys. Radical thought! Life, according to Jane Austen, is actually about living – about doing things, and thinking thoughts, and having experiences, that are as wideranging, interesting and happiness producing as possible.

This means that every now and then you, like her heroines, should take a little break from your obsessive hunt for Mr Darcy, and do other things. It doesn't matter what those things are. Jane herself had all sorts of things she liked doing, not all of them intellectual or high-powered. She loved writing letters. (The more cruel and funnier the better; she once wrote to Cassandra about meeting some mutual acquaintance: 'I was as civil to them as their bad breath would allow.') She loved creating and acting in plays and dramas with her family. She loved travelling and eating. 'I always take care to provide such things as please my own appetite, which I consider as the chief merit in housekeeping,' she once confessed. 'I have had some ragout veal, and I mean to have some haricot mutton tomorrow. We are to kill a pig soon.' She played the piano and thought about fashion. (Of trimming a hat, she wrote to Cassandra: 'I cannot help thinking that it is more natural to have flowers grow out of the head than fruit – what do you think on that subject?') She even loved patchwork – in May 1811 she asked Cassandra, 'Have you remembered to collect peices [sic] for the patchwork? We are now at a standstill.'

The idea behind all these things is that no one great achievement in your life – winning the lottery, getting a promotion, marrying Mr Darcy in a shower of rose petals in a grey stone church with rambling roses over the door – actually makes you happy. Research involving lottery winners in the late 1970s, in fact, showed that six months after their wins, the winners were no happier than they had been before; and the same, incredibly, apparently goes for people who had become paraplegics after accidents; and – I'm betting – for women after marriage. These things may bring great joy or devastation, but it's a temporary emotion. Happiness itself is actually – and this is important – a far more prosaic thing. It is not delivered via a one-off lightning-bolt event; it's accumulated day by day, via a series of small and of-themselves-insignificant things.

Jane is not the only author to understand this. Nancy Mitford, another deeply fantastic woman of letters (who also never married, though she did have a long love affair with a charming and irresponsible Frenchman, Gaston Palewski), had a similar theory. She understood that happiness is like a coral reef, built piece by piece on lots of tiny little things.

Among Nancy's coral polyps of happiness (sorry about 'polyp', awful word) were her beautiful ground-floor flat in Paris, her seasonal Dior fittings, her summer holidays in Venice. These, it could be argued, are hardly little things – but she also loved having gossipy afternoon tea with friends, buying new hats, and finding lovely presents for her godchildren.

And so when heartbreak came – as it inevitably did, of course, because Gaston refused to marry her and eventually married somebody else – she still had this happy life to fall back on, a life she had created independent of him, piece by deliberate piece.

This is exactly what Jane suggests we do. All her heroines get a kick out of their lives (though admittedly, some more than others), completely independent of men. Emma Woodhouse has her music, her visits to the poor and her misguided matchmaking; Elinor Dashwood her drawing, her reading and her love for her mother and sisters; Elizabeth Bennet her chats with Jane and her bracing walks. And this is what we're aiming for, too – a patchwork of interests and pastimes that give us pleasure for their own sake. They don't have to be dynamic or trendy or complex: you don't have to stress about them or get carried away. Just take note of things you really like in your average day, and try to become a little more conscious of them, a little more present to them, and a little more grateful for them. One of my friends, for instance, gets a small but undeniable thrill out of ordering a really nice coffee at her corner cafe each morning and drinking it on the way to work. In this, she's exactly like Jane, who even loved just a quiet seat in a nice room. 'To sit in idleness over a good fire in a well-proportioned room is a luxurious sensation,' she wrote in 1800. Good coffee; high ceilings: that's the sort of thing we're talking about.

There are several benefits to creating your own particular patchwork of happiness in this way. First, and most important, it simply makes you more content, balanced and well-rounded – all good things in and of themselves. Second, it makes you a more interesting person when you *do* meet someone, since you actually have things to talk about, and people who enjoy their own lives are deeply appealing, and make other people want to be part of those lives too. Third, once you actually begin a relationship, and have to pretend you are a well-balanced individual with a rich inner life who does not spend every moment of every day obsessing about said relationship, it helps to have things you like doing that are independent of it. (And further down the relationship track, even after you've stopped obsessing, it's still useful because it gives you something to do when your hero goes off to the pub with the boys, or retreats to the shed to begin construction of his forty-ninth balsawood scale model of a World War I fighter plane.) And, finally, it will help you the way it helped Nancy – when you are trying to get over relationships gone wrong.

A brilliant example of the patchwork of happiness theory is my friend Saska. She called her version the Happy and Whole technique, and as part of it she decided to get fit – an excellent piece of happiness patchwork – and hired a very sexy personal trainer. It all went very well until one morning, when she was running backwards along a jetty under the orders of the sexy personal trainer, and fell off the end of the jetty and into the harbour and broke her toe. Her belief in the theory, however, remained unshaken. 'It's even worth taking notes on little things you find that you really like,' she said, sounding just like Nora Ephron. 'Because sometimes you can't remember them. Oh. And no matter how cute the personal trainer, never run in reverse.'

Another friend of mine bought a flat as a preliminary to meeting her (at that time completely notional) Mr Darcy (who was, of course, going to come and live in the flat with her until they decamped to his enormous ten-bedroom palazzo in Rome), and then discovered that she loved DIY and renovation. She gave up going to nightclubs in favour of the salvage yards; she abandoned internet dating and signed up for a carpentry course. Her flat provided endless pieces of patchwork that made her happy, and she had the good sense to enjoy them to the full. And despite doing exactly the sort of thing our mothers have been suggesting since we were fifteen ('Why don't you join that bushwalking club? You might meet someone who enjoys bushwalking too'), guess who she met when she walked into the first night of Community College Woodworking? That's right. Her personal Mr Darcy, in the living, breathing flesh, with his white shirt rolled up over his tanned forearms and a pencil behind his ear. A Mr Darcy, moreover, who could hardly believe his luck that finally, into his workshop had walked a happy, smiling girl, just dying to find out the difference between mortice-and-tenon joints and dovetail ones. Now the pair of them live in her flat (carpenters, alas, seem not to have much money) and clamp up chair legs in perfect amity all day long.

So there you go. Of course, we would all like the true-love ending to our assiduous building of a happy life. Jane knows this: she knows that our fundamental state of mind is inarguably given a massive boost by finding our particular Darcy/Knightley/Edmund/Wentworth/Carpenter and managing to form a successful relationship with him. There is nothing that brings so much joy, so quickly and simply and gratuitously, as falling – and staying – in love. But she also knows that this emotion is, as John Malkovich put it in the romantic blockbuster *Dangerous Liaisons*, beyond our control. Who knows if and when the carpenter will turn up? (Like the alleged return of another famous carpenter, in fact.) There's really nothing you can do to control that situation. The patchwork of happiness, however, is yours for the making.

DON'T PANIC
20

When you're single, you forget that people in relationships fight. The vision of a relationship is so gleaming with perfection in your mind's eye that you simply can't imagine that every coupled-up person doesn't walk around all day blissed out of their minds by the single, incredible fact that they've found someone to love. It can come as a shock, therefore, to find yourself not only *in* a relationship *with* someone you love, but actually *arguing* with that person, temporarily disliking them intensely, even wishing that they would fall from a great height right on their thoughtless/drunken/non-cleaning/football-obsessed/model-plane-making (delete as appropriate) head.

It will come as a relief to you, should this be the case, to know that Jane Austen heroines fight with their beloveds. Elizabeth Bennet and Mr Darcy are in a state of constant enmity until quite a long way into their relationship; Emma Woodhouse and Mr Knightley are in pretty frequent, albeit usually minor disagreement; and Anne Elliot and Captain Wentworth can be quite snippy with each other (of course, there's eight years of built-up despair and resentment to contend with in their case). Even Fanny Price finds herself occasionally wishing that Edmund would get his shit together and realise Mary Crawford is a total floozy. Of course, being Fanny, her rage is virtually imperceptible to the naked eye, but still, it's there.

Jane has interesting advice to her heroines about arguments. Mostly, she seems to suggest letting them pass without acknowledgement – which, as long as they're not about anything important, is a pretty good strategy, albeit occasionally tricky to implement when you are in a white heat of rage about crumbs on the countertop *again*. But there's a three-point plan you can implement here. 1) Repeat to yourself: 'It is only crumbs on the countertop,' and *resist* the powerful temptation to extrapolate from this to an entire world view in which your hero is constantly careless of your wishes and thoughtless of your comfort and doesn't care about you at all. 2) Remind yourself of a roughly equivalent crime, committed by you – i.e. I leave apple cores by the side of the bed so long they go mouldy. (In fact, the occasional person might argue that mouldy apple cores are far, far worse than crumbs on the counter. But that person would not be me.) 3) Make a note of the crime in a secret place. I don't quite know why you do this. Sometimes it helps to read it back again the next day, realise how puerile it really is, and laugh gaily that it could have bothered you so much. Sometimes, however, it still makes you totally furious even weeks later. Maybe it's some kind of old-crone instinct in which you imagine yourself rubbing your hands over your cauldron and cackling, 'Another heinous crime to combine with my eye of newt and toe of frog . . . one day he shall feel the might of my wrath! Oh, yes he shall! Mwah hah ha ha!' Then you can just get on with your day.

It is a slightly different thing when it's a big argument, over something real. We have two examples of this in Jane's novels: Elizabeth's fight with Darcy after his first proposal; and Emma's argument with Knightley after she is rude to Miss Bates.

The Elizabeth/Darcy altercation is a real humdinger. It's also deeply fantastic, because we see Mr Darcy – who, despite his many perfections, is prone to unappealing arrogance – finally being put in his place by Elizabeth. She starts off by being polite (always a good opening gambit in any argument), but, as he carries on saying completely unhelpful things ('Could you expect me to rejoice in the inferiority of your connections? To congratulate myself on the hope of relations, whose condition in life is so decidedly beneath my own?'), she gets wilder and wilder, culminating in the final, killer blow. 'From the very beginning,' she says, voice dripping with scorn, 'from the first moment I may almost say, of my acquaintance with you, your manners, impressing me with the fullest belief of your arrogance, your conceit, and your selfish disdain of the feelings of others, were such as to form that ground-work of disapprobation, on which succeeding events have built so immoveable a dislike; and I had not known you a month before I felt that *you were the last man in the world whom I could ever be prevailed on to marry.*' [My emphasis!] Wham! Knockout punch. There remains nothing for it but for Darcy to retreat, bloody and beaten, to lick his wounds. And, over time, he realises that these wounds are in fact well-deserved – and so he returns to, metaphorically at least, grovel at Elizabeth's feet and apologise. In the meantime, of course, he also saves Elizabeth's entire family from permanent disgrace, which no doubt helps things along.

So, this gives us one model of heroine argument strategy, but it is predicated on a few things. One, you have to be absolutely sure of your ground. Elizabeth could never have made this fight work to her advantage if she *had* wanted to marry Darcy at the time, or if Darcy *hadn't*, in fact, been a total dickhead. The reality is, there was a completely valid point to be made – i.e. Darcy needing to get his head out of his arse and treat other people, especially people he professed to love, with kindness and sympathy – and Elizabeth managed to make it. Hers was, therefore, a Righteous Anger. And, as God showed everyone in the Old Testament, a Righteous Anger properly deployed is a powerful thing. Two, you've got to be able to stay calm, and keep making valid points. You've got to be like a boxer in the ring – lots of connecting jabs, no wild punches. If you're the sort of heroine who bursts into tears and says things like 'And, anyhow, your model plane is really stupid!' in the middle of an argument about the washing up, Elizabeth's technique is not going to work for you. And three, you've got to be able to think of a devastating parting blow: something that will rankle and smart and ring with truth. If you are someone who can only think of brilliant comeback lines twenty-four hours after the event, forget it.

The second example Jane gives us is for when you, the heroine, are in the wrong. The moment where Knightley dresses down Emma after she's thoughtless and rude to Miss Bates is one of the most brilliantly excruciating scenes in literature; when he says, 'It was badly done, indeed!' I sometimes have to put the book down, hunch my shoulders, block my ears and make a loud humming noise. I can't *bear* it. And neither, of course, can Emma, who is utterly chastened; utterly cast down. She's almost Mr Darcy in reverse: she recognises she's completely in the wrong; she's desperate to make amends; and she realises how much Knightley's opinion really matters to her.

She can't of course, apologise straightaway, because Knightley unhelpfully departs for London. But she's dying to – and when he returns (to confess undying love, as it turns out) she launches into her mea culpa immediately. Interestingly, of course, Knightley is *also* trying to apologise: because he loves Emma, he doesn't want to hurt her, even though his criticism is entirely justified.

And this, really, is what Jane wants us to do in our own hero/heroine arguments. She wants us to avoid them if possible, and try to rise above petty irritations. But if we do get into one, and there's no way out, she wants us to follow the essential guidelines laid down by these examples.

1 SHE WANTS US TO STAY CALM, LIKE BOTH ELIZABETH AND KNIGHTLEY

2 SHE WANTS US TO STICK TO THE POINT – ALSO LIKE ELIZABETH AND KNIGHTLEY

3 SHE WANTS US TO GO AWAY AFTERWARDS AND COOL DOWN, RATHER THAN FIGHTING OURSELVES TO A STANDSTILL

Jane always gives her couples time to calm down after their fights. Not that you need months, like Darcy and Elizabeth get, or even days, like Knightley and Emma. But Jane knows it's impossible to see clearly in the midst of rage; let alone acknowledge fault or seek forgiveness or want to atone. Going away for an hour or two, even to another room – though it's almost unbearable at the time, and every cell in your body is screaming 'Stay and fight! Stay and fight!' – is really worthwhile.

4 DON'T STAND ON CEREMONY WHEN IT COMES TO APOLOGISING

This is a massive sticking point in most arguments, usually because there isn't a clear indication as to who should do the apologising, and it feels *hard* to be the one when you're still smarting from the argument itself. Being the first to say sorry feels like you're giving ground, or somehow admitting you were wrong. But, no, says Jane: apologising is actually the smart strategic move, because you immediately gain moral ascendancy and a big metaphorical tick beside your name; and your other half knows this, and (usually, alas, silently) acknowledges it, and is massively relieved you've done it first.

And remember you're not apologising for your *view* (unless you are wildly in the wrong, which as we know is virtually unheard of in the case of heroines), just for the argument itself. 'I'm sorry about our argument,' is all you usually need, not 'I'm sorry I raised the fact that you sound like a mastodon when you chew.' And if you really love the person, you really *will* be sorry you've been arguing, so this approach has the added advantage of being true.

5 ALWAYS REMEMBER THIS BUSINESS OF LOVE

Fundamentally, this person we are screaming at is the person we love, and we don't really, in our heart of hearts, want to hurt them. We want them to do/stop doing/change/recognise something, but we don't want to crush their spirit and make them hate us. For Jane's heroines, arguments always lead somewhere. In the end, after much difficulty and soul-searching, they make things better for both Elizabeth and Emma. And, as Jane Austen heroines, we should bear this in mind. We should argue with a view to making things better. We should never lose our vision of a more beautiful, crumbless – even, dare it be said, apple-coreless – world.

THE DEVASTATING SILENCE
21

Our own ceaseless Mr Darcy quest notwithstanding, we are all occasionally asked to give advice about other people's love lives – usually those of our girlfriends, female relations, and random gay men we meet in nightclubs at 4 a.m. This can, of course, be enormous fun: the opportunity to indulge in a full-on, no-holds barred (especially if it's a gay man telling you the story) exploration of someone else's emotional saga. It's fantastic. And it's also a blessed relief to listen to all the ways someone *else* is: a) stuffing up their lives, b) totally miserable being single, c) failing to realise the man they're in love with is a complete bastard.

But Jane is very wary about the wisdom of giving other people advice about romance and relationships (this book, which is clearly a model of tact and diplomacy, excepted), especially if that advice involves saying some version of the words: 'This person you're with is a total moron.' When this is the case, we long to tell our friends and loved ones what we think, and advise them to run, run, run for the hills. Loyalty, we feel, demands it; justice, friendship and our own moral code make it imperative that we stand up and speak the truth. Surely our friends would want us to be honest? In their position, wouldn't we want the people who love us to tell us how things really are?

In a word, no. Jane is absolutely against pointing out how obnoxious other people's boyfriends/lovers/husbands/occasional shags are. There are two reasons for this. One is the pragmatic reality that any advice that doesn't exactly correspond to the listener's own desires is going to be ignored anyhow.[20] Jane knows this, and her feeling is: don't waste your breath. And secondly, Jane believes, like our first-grade teachers, that if you can't say something nice, you shouldn't say anything at all. So no telling our work colleague that the courier girl clearly isn't interested in him; or our gay mate that the boy in the nightclub who he's been shimmying in front of for the past four hours looks, well, straight. And if our friend raises the topic himself – as in 'Do you think he might be straight?' we should just smile beatifically and speak of other things.

---

[20] As Patrick O'Brian, author of the best series of sea novels ever written, puts it in *The Reverse of the Medal*: 'He knew that in cases of this kind any advice that did not exactly agree with the wishes of those concerned was always useless and often offensive.'

Of course, Jane recognises that the desire to '*say* something' is a very human impulse. Elizabeth can't help but express her incredulity to Charlotte Lucas about the fact that she's marrying Mr Collins, for example. 'Engaged to Mr Collins! My dear Charlotte – impossible!' This clearly hurts Charlotte, whose face falls 'on receiving so direct a reproach', but who then replies calmly (and with a little flash of steel), 'Why should you be surprised, my dear Eliza – Do you think it incredible that Mr Collins should be able to procure any woman's good opinion, because he was not so happy as to succeed with you?' And Elizabeth, recognising that she has broken the unspoken pact on such matters, has to pull herself very swiftly together to prevent a further breach. So even if you have, like Lizzie, the angel of truth on your side, it serves no purpose to speak out.

In *Persuasion*, meanwhile, we see even more terrible consequences of forthright opinion-giving. Anne Elliot is persuaded by her friend and confidante Lady Russell not to marry the dashing young sea officer Frederick Wentworth. Listen, says Lady Russell, this is a disaster. This Wentworth dude is sexy as hell, I grant you. But he's young, he's broke, and the sea is fickle. He might be killed or thrown on the beach without a ship at any moment. Spanish treasure galleons are notoriously hard to come by these days: he might continue piddling along as a lieutenant for the rest of his life without two gold coins to rub together. You're young, you're gorgeous, you're the daughter of a baronet. You can do a lot better than him.

Anne, who's only nineteen at the time, listens to her. Big mistake. She then has to endure eight years of misery, during which she loses her looks, becomes a spinster, and lives at the beck and call of her hellish family. It all ends happily, thank goodness, but you're struck all the time with how close to disaster Anne has come: all thanks to the well-meaning but wildly off-base advice of her friend.

So back off, says Jane. Your advice might also be well meaning; it might be delivered with love; it might even be true. But you mustn't say a word. You must smile through gritted teeth, let your friends make their own mistakes, and learn the value of a devastating silence.

One last thing about this rule – it also works in reverse. That is, you shouldn't say anything wildly complimentary either. This seems cruel, I know, and it's admittedly more murky territory: if you really like someone's new man you should certainly say so. But, as with all things, Jane would argue for moderation. Along with the Dalai Lama – with whom I feel sure she would have had a great deal in common – Jane believed in the middle way. Be enthusiastic if you feel enthusiastic, but don't overdo it. 'That Peter Pan seems very nice,' you might say. 'I like his jaunty cap.' Then just leave it at that. Anything more, and you don't know what impact your words might have.

THE DEVASTATING SILENCE

Poor Jane herself had a perfect example of this in real life. She had a niece, Fanny Knight, who had a suitor. Jane thought said suitor was very nice, and wrote warmly about him to Fanny, saying what a lovely man he was. The next thing she knew, Fanny (who actually wasn't sure if she loved the suitor) had nevertheless relied on Jane's opinion and agreed to marry him.

Jane was appalled. 'You frighten me out of my wits by your reference[!]' she wrote to Fanny. 'Indeed you must not let anything depend on my opinion[!] Your own feelings & none but your own, should determine such an important point[!] . . . I dare not say "Determine to accept him[!]" The risk is too great for *you*, unless your own sentiments prompt it[!]'[21]

Fanny, of course, sounds like a fool – even if your aunt *was* Jane Austen, marrying someone purely on her say-so is ridiculous. But Jane had learnt her lesson. As far as possible within the bounds of common friendship and affection, when it comes to other people's relationships, it's better for everyone if you can preserve a judicious silence. You may hear evil, you may see evil – but better for everyone concerned if you speak no evil at all.

---

21 My exclamation marks. Jane was far too cool to use exclamation marks, but you know she wanted to.

MARRIAGE

22

There comes a time in the affairs of coupled-up Jane Austen heroines when you have to ask the big question. What next? What next with this real-life boyfriend/companion/Austenesque hero? Do you want to marry him – or at least commit to some kind of shared-duvet-and-steak-knives life together? Does he want the same with you?

Exactly who a heroine should marry is, perhaps, the most fundamental question Jane Austen ever asks – which is convenient for us, since it's also the most fundamental question *we* ever ask, at least on the subject of anyone we're dating.

It's also a question, incidentally, that Jane Austen asked herself. When she was twenty, Jane herself *may*[22] have fallen in love with a young Irishman called Tom Lefroy. He was

---

[22] The primary source material for this relationships consists of a couple of letters, written by Jane herself, filled with self-deprecating irony.

visiting the neighbourhood; he met Jane; they danced and talked and teased each other about Tom Jones (the abolitionist, as opposed to the Welsh crooner). 'I am almost afraid to tell you how my Irish friend and I behaved,' she writes to Cassandra in early 1796. 'Imagine to yourself everything most profligate and shocking in the way of dancing and sitting down together . . . He has but one fault, which time will, I trust, entirely remove – it is that his morning coat is a great deal too light.'

As it turned out, Jane never got the chance to see Lefroy in a darker coat; let alone decide whether she loved him or wanted to marry him, because he was whisked away by his relatives to what turned out to be a highly successful career in the law.[23] But she never speaks with the same lightness and excitement about another man again. And in her fictional world, marriage is the natural end point of everything. Elizabeth Bennet and Mr Darcy, Jane Bennet and Bingley, Emma and Mr Knightley, Anne Elliot and Captain Wentworth, Marianne Dashwood and Colonel Brandon, Eleanor Dashwood and Edward Ferrars, Fanny Price and Edmund Bertram – the

---

23 To this day, nobody really knows – though everyone feverishly speculates – how Jane felt about this. Was she in love with Lefroy? Was she devastated when he left Hampshire? (He eventually married well, had several children, and became Lord Chief Justice of Ireland, so clearly for him, life struggled on – though he did say, in his dotage, that he had been in love with Jane.) Or was the whole interlude merely a harmless flirtation, which provided Jane with good copy for an anecdote?

list goes on and on. Every heroine, every character Jane cares about, achieves matrimony by the end of her stories.

Of course, marriage is one thing. But these days, some heroines don't get married. They may live forever with their particular Mr Darcys without actually tying the knot. So although for Jane the question is 'How does a heroine know who's the right man to marry?', here in the new millennium, the equivalent version of the question is 'How do I know that this man is *the one*? The one I want to live with, and perhaps have children with; the one whose toenails I will be willing to clip when he is bald and demented and keeps throwing his dentures in the bin.' Marriage itself may be part of the deal, or it may not.

Either way, the key to the question is love. But love in what way, and to what degree? As Tina Turner asks so percipiently (that's Tina, always grappling with the big existential questions): 'What's Love Got To Do With It?'

In Jane's day, virtually nothing. Marriage was sometimes about expediency (as with Wickham and Lydia Bennet: it's either marriage or ruin), often about social position (Maria Bertram, marrying hopeless Rushworth), and always, always about cold, hard cash. 'As to fortune, it is a most eligible match,' points out Jane Bennet of Charlotte Lucas and the hideous Mr Collins. And Charlotte herself agrees. 'I am not romantic, you know,' she tells Elizabeth almost apologetically. 'I never was. I ask only a comfortable home.'

Jane Austen, of course, knows this attitude first hand, and as a pragmatist, she can see the point. She knows, from her own life experience and that of her friends, that marriage is one of many women's very, very few options to save them from poverty. She recognises the dilemma – and the potentially mutually exclusive relationship – between true love on the one hand, and a comfortable life on the other. As do we all, of course. Who among us hasn't had a beloved girlfriend – a woman whose judgement we implicitly trust under normal circumstances (yes, you can eat that mushroom; no, you light it from *that* end) – suddenly decide to marry someone we think is a total dickhead? We know she's been single for a long time; we know she wants kids, but it still comes as a shock that one day, suddenly, she's married to an idiot.

This is known in Jane Austen circles as 'making the Charlotte Lucas choice'. Charlotte Lucas – not beautiful, with a foolish father and no fortune – must find a husband if she's to avoid becoming both poor and a spinster: two fates apparently (I use the word advisedly) worse than death. And, ergo, she marries Mr Collins.

A modern version of this is Lori Gottlieb's Mr Good Enough. Lori Gottleib, who wrote *Marry Him: The Case for Settling for Mr Good Enough*, is a tireless advocate for the Mr Collinses of this world. Her basic premise is that, if we want a reliable life partner and children, we should abandon our dreams of the ten out of ten KISA (Knight In Shining

Armour – i.e. Mr Darcy) and accept Mr Six out of Ten – he of the bad breath, the dumb jokes, and the painful personal habits, but also of the goodish job, the consistent kindness, and the coinciding family values – before we ourselves get so old and haggard that we can only attract a five out of ten (criminal record, one tooth, wooden leg).

A wooden leg, one can't help thinking, would come as a blessed relief compared to Mr Collins' endlessly unspooling inanities. Would Jane really have us make the Charlotte Lucas choice? Abandon any hint of romance and genuine emotional attachment and hook up with the nearest man who has some cash, a nice house, and not an ounce of sense in his head?

No. Jane does give Charlotte Lucas – otherwise trapped by the social constraints of her time – Mr Collins. But she shows what she thinks of such a choice by making Mr Collins as ridiculous as humanly possible. No woman, she wants to say, should have to do what Charlotte did – it's an indictment on the social system, on gender relations, on us all.

It's not, importantly, an indictment on Charlotte herself, however. Jane recognises that Charlotte took one of the very few avenues open to her, and made her choice calmly, with dignity and honesty. And so Jane leaves her in peace, and even gives her a measure of quiet contentment: a lovely house in the countryside with the rooms so arranged that she sometimes barely sees Mr Collins 'between breakfast and dinner'.

But the fact remains that this is not Jane Austen's choice for any of her heroines. What she really wants, unequivocally, is for us to marry – or choose our life partners – for love. *All* her heroines marry for love: it's as if Jane can't bear for them not to. Her novels, remember, are classics of the true-love genre. She makes it absolutely clear that Elizabeth would never have married Darcy if she hadn't loved him – however appealing his various assets. Anne Elliot refuses Mr Elliot, and Fanny won't have Henry Crawford, either: both good worldly choices for these heroines, but devoid of love.

Indeed, there's an even clearer example. In real life, Jane herself refused to make the Charlotte Lucas choice: she turned down a materially advantageous offer of marriage because she didn't love the offerer.

Harris Bigg-Wither[24] was the young brother of Jane's old friends, Althea and Catherine. On 2 December 1803, when Jane was visiting his sisters at the family estate, he proposed to her. He was wealthy, he was well-connected, he had plenty of cash: in nineteenth-century terms, he was a fantastic catch for Jane, who was five years older, had not published a novel, and had an allowance of fifty pounds a year.[25] Perhaps that's why she initially accepted his offer that

---

24 I know. Almost impossible to believe. But I kid you not. Alas, history does not relate whether Mr Bigg-Wither actually had, you know, large thighs.
25 Roughly £1600 in today's money.

fateful evening. Marriage to Harris would make her mistress of a large Hampshire house and estate; it would allow her to ensure her parents' and Cassandra's comfort for the rest of their lives; she would be surrounded by sisters-in-law she loved and her own family. But Harris was unintellectual, and he had nothing in common with her in terms of interests or instinctive sympathy. And she did not love him. The following morning she withdrew her acceptance, despite the wild embarrassment and awkwardness it must have caused everyone involved. And so we see that in her own life – despite the very real threats of poverty, humiliation and social failure – marriage without love proved an impossible proposition. She can do no less for her heroines – and we can do no less for ourselves.

None of Jane's heroes are perfect, but their heroines genuinely love them. And by love, Jane means something quite specific. These women have found men they respect and admire – 'esteem' is her word – that they like and feel some sense of kindred spiritedness to, and that they fancy and find physically exciting. (This is, admittedly, harder to spot in some cases than others: Fanny and Edmund, for instance, are the two most staid 20-somethings it's possible to imagine. But Elizabeth and Darcy are clearly dying to rip each other's clothes off.)

So as for as settling for Mr Good Enough, à la Lori Gottlieb, Jane Austen's heroines don't do it, and neither should we. They always end up with their ten out of ten man – the one who, given all the world, they would still have chosen for themselves. But here's the crucial point. These men are the *heroines'* number tens, not objective examples of masculine perfection. Okay, okay – Darcy does come close, but even he is arrogant and reserved and might not be the most comfortable of husbands; Knightley is terribly bossy and Wentworth overly sanguine; Edmund (as already mentioned) staid and earnest. These are not perfect men. But the heroines take the rough with the smooth, and love them anyway.

So this is how we can have our Lori Gottlieb cake and eat it too. We can pick men who are right for us. They won't be perfect men, and we should give up on this ideal. They will not have Robert Pattinson's jaw line or Prince William's real estate or Bill Gates' fortune, and we should work hard to rid ourselves of these kinds of expectations. They will be real men, with real flaws, just as we are real women, who may sometimes (though of course very rarely) fall short of perfection ourselves. But in no way should we 'settle' for a man we know we don't love (i.e. admire, respect, like and fancy) because we don't think we'll find anyone better. My God. Life – let alone marriage – is hard enough, without adding Mediocre Man to the mix. As Jane herself proved, it's far better, more cheerful and more successful to be on your own.

BABIES
23

Having babies, clearly, is something people – even heroines – occasionally do. And so, since Jane is concerned with the full tapestry of human experience, we can be sure she was interested in when, why and how heroines should have them.

Not that any of her heroines actually *does* have a baby in the novels – then we'd be dealing not only with interest, but horrified scandal and public condemnation, given that they're all unmarried. (Poor Eliza Williams, Willoughby's dupe, does give birth to a daughter, and though we only hear about it very peripherally, it's a tale of total woe from start to finish.)

Still. In life, Jane Austen had an unusual relationship to children. Firstly, she had none of her own – which made her one of a very select group in eighteenth-century Europe, since virtually every ovulating female had no option but to produce offspring or (literally) die in the attempt. The almost universal habit of marriage for women, and the entirely universal lack of reasonable contraception (note that I am disqualifying anything involving sheep's intestine or iron padlocks as reasonable) meant that everyone was having children, everywhere, all the time. Except Jane – and Cassandra, her sister and closest friend. This removes Jane from the life of female childbearing so common to her contemporaries, and brings her far closer to women of our age, with our delayed childbearing and our increasing numbers of heroines who don't have kids at all.

She did, of course, have lots of brothers, most of whom procreated wildly; particularly Edward Austen Knight, who was adopted by rich relatives and inherited their estate. He had a slightly painful-sounding wife, Elizabeth, who was constantly giving birth; and both Jane and Cassandra were called upon with monotonous regularity to go and 'help' when she popped another one. Actually, Cassandra was called more often than Jane, which makes one wonder if perhaps there wasn't much love lost between Elizabeth and Jane; or whether something about Jane's personality – humour, cynicism, the tendency to eye roll, maybe? – wasn't all that conducive to childbed sympathy. 'Mary grows rather more reasonable about her Child's beauty,' she wrote to Cassandra in 1799 of another sister-in-law, '& says that she does not think him really handsome, but I suspect her moderation . . .'

But that doesn't mean Jane didn't like children. Indeed, as we've discussed, she seems to have really enjoyed them, especially when they got old enough to enjoy a joke. And she, like most of us, was not immune to the charms of a small chubby person who took a shine to her. 'My dear itty Dordy's remembrance of me is very pleasing to me,' she wrote to Cassandra of her little nephew George. 'Kiss him for me.'

So what does all this mean for her view on being a heroine who is having a baby? Well, two women do have babies in the course of her books: Mrs Weston and Mrs Charlotte Palmer, an acquaintance of Elinor Dashwood's. Mrs Palmer is a fool, though a very cheerful one, and it seems that her unshakeable good humour will help her in maternal as well as marital life. (Marital life involves the certified fun-wrecker Mr Palmer, so things can hardly get worse.) But Mrs Weston is certainly a heroine – albeit a minor one – and her baby is the cause of great joy and interest for Emma, so in general, the ruling seems to be thumbs up. Having a baby is a good thing.

But she's refreshingly sane about it. In our current social set-up, having babies has been elevated to some sort of holy vocation; some mysterious rite that takes women to a higher plane and without which the voyage of their lives is bound in shallows and in miseries. There is immense pressure of the oh-poor-childless-you-who-will-never-know-the-true-rich-meaning-of-life sort on women these days, which has the power to make those of us without children feel terrible and bereft and missing-out-ish, even if giving birth to a watermelon and having another human being maul fluid out of our boobs for twelve months is *not* our idea of a good time. For those of us who in fact long for these things, meanwhile, this pressure can be utterly devastating.

To all of which Jane would say: 'Don't beat yourself up.' Having a baby is all very well; but it's not the be all and end all of life. There are all sorts of ways to be happy without a baby; babies are not prerequisites for a good life. They are, of course, one of the great adventures in life, but so is writing a great novel or six, or moving to Borneo and living in a treetop holiday home where the orangutans come and share your morning banana. You have some adventures, and not others: that's how life goes.

And if the whole baby thing is absolutely top of your list of adventures-that-must-be-had-and-I-don't-give-a-shit-about-orangutans, then Jane, ever the pragmatist, would say: 'Take control of your life and have one.' If the only reason you haven't had one is because you haven't met your Mr Darcy, and time is marching on, think about whether you want to have the sadness of missing out on a child be added to the sadness of not having met the man of your dreams. We tend to link these desires: I want a-man-and-a-baby. Which is fair enough: centuries (like the one Jane grew up in) of cultural indoctrination have conditioned us to this conflation. But thanks to the myriad blessings of the modern world, we no longer have to fall into this if-not-one-then-neither trap. You can, today, have a baby without a man. There are sperm banks and gorgeous gay best friends and entire, increasingly mainstream industries set up to help you do so: there's legislation, financial protection and proper health care. Stand up, take responsibility for your maternal desire, separate it – if need be – from your Darcy-desire, and take action.

One note here. There comes a time in the affairs of single heroines who long for babies when it can seem like a good idea to just have sex with *someone, anyone,* in order to have a baby, regardless of the man in question and how he might feel about it; indeed, regardless of whether he even knows it's happening at all. And it's worth entering a plea from Jane to all heroines: don't do it. Don't use a man as an unknowing sperm donor. It's a breathtaking deception, and it's fundamentally unfair to everyone involved. No, no, no, no, no!

And another note. Even if you *do* have a partner, a beloved, a genuine Mr Darcy, don't just stop using contraception and try to fall pregnant if he's not on board with the whole baby idea. This is just as bad, and no amount of he-will-love-it-when-it-happens-he'll-come-round-he's-just-being-a-man reasoning justifies it. It is categorically unjustifiable. It's a bit like saying to your boyfriend: 'Darling, I'd like a new car, and I'd like you to give me $20,000 to buy it,' and him saying, 'No, I don't think I want a new car at the moment,' and you hacking into his bank account and taking the money anyway. Actually, it's way worse than that – and you would never do that, would you? No. So don't do this either.

So there you go. If you do have a baby, either on your own, or with someone you love who wants one too, Jane would say what she'd say to any heroine boarding a vessel that was carrying her across the high seas to a deeply thrilling, reasonably perilous new life. It's what my uncle Arthur, born in 1900, used to say before setting off on any adventure that would take him beyond the boundary fence of his isolated country sheep farm. 'Lay all your clothes, and all your money, out on the bed,' he'd say. 'Then halve your clothes, and double your money.' And then do what Captain Chesley B. Sullenberger III told the passengers of US Airways flight 1549 when they were about to crash into the Hudson River. (I feel sure he and Uncle Arthur would have got on famously.) Brace! Brace! Brace!

THE HIDEOUS BREAK-UP

24

Not every love story ends happily ever after. If it did, life would in fact *be* a Jane Austen novel, and we would have no need of the novels themselves. But at some point, all relationships follow one of two paths. We've discussed the marriage/long-term commitment path, leaving only the alternative, which is, well, the path to doom and disaster.

This doesn't sound terribly upbeat, I grant you. And it would be remiss of me not to acknowledge that sometimes, when relationships end, we skip from the wreckage with a song in our hearts and a jig in our steps, blessedly grateful to be released. But that's not the relationship end we're talking about here. What we have in mind is how the Jane Austen heroine should deal with loss, not of Wickham, but of Mr Darcy himself. What do we do when the Jane Austen hunt goes horribly, horribly wrong?

Getting over someone you've really loved can be hard to do. Jane knows this better than anybody: if you accept that in real life she was in love with Tom Lefroy as a twenty-year-old, as already discussed, you might also accept that she turned down Harris Bigg-Wither seven years later, at least in part, because she hadn't got over Tom. And her sister Cassandra, despite being only twenty-four when her fiancé perished of yellow fever in the Caribbean (as fiancés were depressingly wont to do in the eighteenth century, especially when they were penniless clergymen ministering to troops in the Napoleonic Wars), never took an interest in another man, remaining single for the rest of her days. As well as these two demoralising examples from life, in Jane's fiction, Anne Elliot is so far from being over Wentworth when he reappears after eight years that she's incapable of speech in his presence, which doesn't augur well for the wholeness of her heart. And let's not even get into Marianne Dashwood's state of mind after Willoughby dumps her. She can't eat, she can't sleep, she can barely speak. All she can do is weep with agony.

In a radical departure from our normal practice – i.e. to be as much like Jane and Jane's heroines as humanly possible, given the restrictions of the space–time continuum, the march of history, and the sad lack of figured muslin in the twenty-first century world – I think in this case we must follow Jane's example by opposition, not emulation. We want no modern Jane Austen heroines wandering around alone and palely loitering a decade after a relationship falls apart. We want them back out there on the dating bandwagon, in pursuit of truth, justice, and the triumph of happiness.

What we often fail to realise is that getting over relationships is an act of *will*. It is a decision we make. Of course, time alone is a great healer: however sunk in a slough of despond you are; however determined to preserve the memory of your love between hot-pressed leaves of rose-tinted paper for ever more, the action of time wears away everything in the end, until eventually, all that remains are the lone and level sands stretching far away. Shelley wasn't right about everything – in fact, you might argue he was right about very little, especially when it came to women – but he was right about that.

The point in this case, of course, is that we don't want to be waiting for the deserts of vast eternity to finally blow in and bury the monument of our love. We want to get free of it, get past it, get to the point of being ready to love again. And to do that, we must *decide* to get over it. As Elinor Dashwood puts it to Marianne: 'The composure of mind with which I have brought myself at present to consider the . . . [apparent loss of Edward Ferrars] has been the effect of constant and painful exertion.'

In pursuit of this composure, however, the Jane Austen heroine should be kind to herself. Don't expect to get over someone you've genuinely loved for ages. Ages and *ages*. Of course if it's just a Wickham/Elizabeth, Frank Churchill/Emma style dalliance, in which your heart was never truly, madly, deeply engaged, you might be surprised – even embarrassed – at how quickly you bounce back, especially if you make an active choice to try. But if you really loved someone – if you thought they were your one and only Knightley in shining armour – it's going to take a long, long time.

So take it gently. Spas, massages and pedicure treatments are all deeply relevant here – so much so that they should be on some sort of health rebate scheme: if you can prove you've suffered a romantic reversal in the previous twelve months, you should be entitled to an 85 per cent refund.

Getting your hair cut can also be good, but be careful. My hairdresser, who has known me for fourteen years, once refused to cut my hair at all after I told him I'd just broken up with a boyfriend. Admittedly, I'd gone in with hair past my shoulders, carrying a picture of someone tonsorially resembling Sinead O'Connor, so this may have been a red flag. As he pointed out to me, it is a little known but important fact that unless you have an unusually beautiful, smoothly moulded skull, baldness is not a good option.

Talk to your friends and family – but be careful here, too. Avoid anyone that wants to help you, or encourage you, to dwell on the past, rehash the ending, or imagine a miraculous reunion. Talk to people who are sympathetic, who genuinely love you, and who are optimistic about the future. Let them organise things to distract you – activities, dinners, nights out. But probably not dates, at least not until you've passed the watershed of making it through a whole day without crying.

Don't worry about the crying, incidentally. Before you break up with someone – when you are heart-whole and, well, normal – crying in public seems like one of those unimaginable things: every now and then you see someone doing it and you just think '*How?* How can that person be so *abandoned*?' And then your heart is broken and you cry everywhere, everywhere, everywhere. I remember during one break-up I kept a kind of mental list: I cried in every room at home (the bathroom was especially good, because the acoustics are great and you can get a properly resonant wail going, without anyone hearing you. Plus you can see yourself in the mirror, which adds to the self-pitying horror of it all. *Plus* it's easy to clean up afterwards, since you just stand in the shower till the snot's gone), in the office loos, in my boss's office, at my desk, in the lift, in the lobby, in the office garden, on the bus, on the street, in cars, while running, while walking, on the beach. I cried on my own and with all my friends; with work people, and with total strangers. Oddly, there's something reassuring about crying among strangers, because unless you look like you're actually about to kill yourself – *actually* throw yourself under the train or over the escalator or in front of the bus – they tend to leave you alone, so you don't have to explain anything, but at the same time they all look terribly sympathetic. So you get the concern, without the interaction, when the interaction is too much to bear. The best place of all to cry, by the way, is the pub: because there's always alcohol at hand, and there's no better excuse for drinking than tears.

So let yourself cry. Let yourself weep and wail and gnash your teeth and rend your clothes and tear your hair: let your inner Marianne Dashwood really cut loose. Give yourself one month.[26] And then, the day after the one-month anniversary of your break-up, channel Winston Churchill and take a stand. Go into the bathroom, look in the mirror, and say, 'I am now going to start getting over this. This is not the end of feeling terrible. It is not even the beginning of the end. But it is, perhaps, the end of the beginning.' It's at this point that you re-enter the lists of your Jane Austen heroine world, and the rest of your life can begin.

---

[26] An alternative, three-month strategy was once suggested by Garrison Keillor, creator of the fantastic Lake Wobegon novels and radio show, and former Mr Blue agony-uncle for salon.com. Here it is: 'Get a haircut and buy some new duds. Cut out alcohol and put yourself on a diet of greens and fruit. Hurl yourself into profitable activity: read a book a week, enrol in a French class, memorize poetry, go to the gym daily. Do this for ninety days, and at the end of it, sit down and ask yourself how you feel about your life. Ninety days of self-improvement fuelled by anger should use up much of your anger, and then you can have the final revenge, which is to forgive the pitiful bastard and get on with your life.' Jane Austen would be all for it.

STAYING FRIENDS - HAH!
25

Jane, as we're discovering, is interesting on the subject of relationships that go horribly wrong. She is not really terrific on the I-will-survive recovery phase of heroine behaviour, possibly because she didn't have enough Gloria Gaynor in her life.

But we can extrapolate. Imagine, for a moment, that things had collapsed in a ball of flames with Mr Darcy and Elizabeth Bennet, despite their mutual happiness and the 'That's it, I've found the one, Gloria in excelsis Deo!' moment (and let's face it, most relationships that end in tears begin with these things). Can you imagine the two of them ever getting together for a casual coffee on Sunday afternoon? Catching a movie on Thursday night? Even chatting on the phone once or twice a week?

No. Me either. The sad truth is that *it is impossible to be friends with people you have just broken up with*. I know this goes against the very foundations of many women's relationship belief system, but believe me, grasshopper, I speak the truth. It is impossible. Always, Always, Always.

You think it's all okay. You think you don't still have feelings for Mr Once-was-love-of-your-life. You think you are genuinely friends: that you care about each other in a platonic, altruistic, almost familial fashion. *This is a lie.*

What is really going on is that you are attempting to assuage the ache of Mr O's absence in your life with what amounts, in fact, to a kind of pseudo-relationship. The pseudo-relationship is something Jane does know about. (Lucy Steele's vulgar sister Anne is conducting a full-blown pseudo-relationship with the mysterious Dr Davies for most of *Sense and Sensibility*.) But while you're busily engaged in having a non-relationship relationship in your head, Mr O is doing one of any number of things, none of which are going to work out for you. He could be being friends with you because he still fancies you and there's the possibility of break-up sex (very bad for you). Or he could be a deeply caring guy, who genuinely likes you, and is trying to be friends with you because this seems to be the nicest way of handling the situation. (This happens more often than you might think, and is lovely, but still hopeless for you.) Or, finally, he could still be in love with you (usually only an issue if you're the one who has ended the relationship), but then you *still* shouldn't be friends with the poor guy, because everything I'm saying about you then applies to *him*.

Despite these truths, however, many of us still persist, like lemmings plunging over the cliff, down the pseudo-relationship path to our inevitable doom. Why does this happen? Well, perhaps because you can't bear the agony of not having Mr O in your life at all; or because you have a control-freakish, deeply masochistic desire to know what he's doing and how he's feeling and who he's seeing; or, lastly (and most commonly), because you think, in your heart of hearts, that you're going to somehow convince him that you are far more fantastic than he ever realised and he's going to have an epiphany, realise he's made a terrible mistake, and try to win you back.

Sigh.

So. You form the pseudo-relationship. You tell yourself it's fine and that everything's okay and you're 'just friends', but all you are doing is storing up a *whole new world of pain* for yourself. And you will have to contend with this pain further down the track, when you realise that you actually aren't friends – not really. You might truly care about each other, but you are not friends. Your interests are in fundamental conflict. And usually the moment you realise this – the moment when the pseudo-relationship spectacularly collapses – is when Mr O blows you off for a hot date, or (God forbid) starts going out with someone new, or in some other way signals to you that he no longer thinks of you the way the 'friendship' has allowed you to keep thinking of him – i.e. as the love interest in your life.

The only solution to extracting yourself from the pseudo-relationship is the no-contact rule. This is also a rule Jane understands. Even Marianne Dashwood, *finally*, after much operatic melodrama and screaming and carrying on like a pork chop, gives Willoughby's letters to Elinor and resolves (sort of) to get on with her life. The no-contact rule involves, surprisingly, removing yourself from all possible contact with the man in question. Do not call him; do not text him; do not semaphore him from the roof of your apartment building. Do not go where he goes; do not ask about him; do not let mutual friends tell you what he's doing. I know how difficult this is if you have a wide circle of friends or social activities in common. Make a huge effort. Unfriend him on Facebook; stop following him on Twitter; tell your friends you don't want to hear about him. Try to figure out your social schedule so you're not in the same place as he is at the same time; focus on manifesting the best version of Jane Bennet's serenity and dignity. If necessary, you can even tell him, calmly, that you're going to give yourself a break from contact, so you won't be in touch for a while.

A note on this conversation. If you are the kind of heroine who needs things to be very clear, relationship-wise, it's always worth having the closure conversation either when you end the relationship, or at some point in the aftermath. This is slightly but crucially different from the actual *end-of-relationship* conversation, which often happens at a pretty emotional moment, even for the most self-controlled heroine. The *closure* conversation usually comes once the dust has settled and all the screaming is over, and its purpose is to clarify the fact that things are indeed over, and set out the terms for future contact. Which are, of course, zero – until some impossibly distant future point where you really, genuinely don't give a damn. As always, dignity is the key. Expressing love and gratitude are okay. 'I really loved you, and I had a great time with you, and I'm really sorry things didn't work out.' Justifiable, controlled anger is also okay. 'I'm sorry, there really was no excuse for the chimpanzee. But I hope things work out well for you in the circus.' So are clear, easily understood directives. 'Never call me again. I do not like you or respect you. The very thought of hearing your oddly high-pitched voice makes my blood run cold.' What is not okay is: 'I hope we can still be friends.' Maybe you can, but not now, not soon, not at any time you need to worry about at this point. If he makes the friend request to you, say: 'Maybe. But not yet. And in the meantime, please don't call me or make contact in any way.'

Once you've had the closure conversation (or, in its absence, made your own decision that the case really *is*, as it were, *closed*) it will feel like you've amputated a limb. You will then immediately, and possibly for some time afterwards, want desperately to go places where he is in the hope that he will see you and feel devastated (cue epiphany, change of heart, and that whole ball of wax again). But this misses the point, which is how devastated such sightings will make *you* feel: churned up, adrenalised and grief-stricken all at once. This can almost be better than the horrible ache of loss you feel the rest of the time. But it's like an awful drug experience or alcohol binge. It may feel energising, even hectically enjoyable at the time. But the comedown is never, ever worth the hit.

So grit your teeth and get out of his orbit. Recruit every ounce of your Jane Bennet/Elinor Dashwood self-control and sense of pride, and move your life away from his. Pride is valuable here – it's pride that will (hopefully, or at least after a certain point) stop you shamelessly pumping your friends for information, or hanging round the places he goes like some kind of lovelorn wet mop. Do whatever you need to do to distract yourself in the meantime: travel to some far pavilion; take up some terrifying death-defying activity like skydiving that you would never previously have so much as considered but that now, since you actually don't care whether you live or die, holds no fear for you; become an expert in French knotting and satin-stitch embroidery.

Sometimes a time frame helps. Three months. Cut out all contact for three months, then see how you feel. Chances are, you'll still feel pretty devastated. But you'll also feel better. You'll have maintained your self-respect; you won't have used his presence to inflict more pain on yourself; you will have stopped him actively hurting you by knowing about his dating or shagging or meeting other women. You never know – you might even have met another man. (A rebound man, perchance! Oh happy day!) If you really loved Mr O, this is incredibly unlikely, but at least if you're not using up 99 per cent of your emotional energy telling yourself you're 'just friends' with the former love of your life, you might have something available for someone new.

All these things can happen with the benefit of space and time. Space is what you give yourself by not pretending that you're friends. Time is what God, or the universe, or the great revolution of the karmic wheel gives you. And when the wheel turns, and you can re-enter the world with your head high, your dignity intact, and fifteen firescreens elaborately embroidered, it will all be worthwhile.

PRESERVE YOUR DIGNITY
26

So, we've discussed making the decision to get over Mr Once-was-fabulous, being kind to yourself, and cutting off contact. Of course, we've done so in the full knowledge Jane's business was not really *with* break-ups or their aftermath; her whole gig was with the sophisticated, beautifully dovetailed happy ending.

The crucial thing about this, for our modern-day purposes, is that Jane's characters never really have to deal with the whole actually-I-know-I-said-I-loved-you-but-I've-sort-of-decided-that-I-don't-so-now-I'm-going-to-ride-off-into-the-wild-blue-yonder-and-leave-you-here-with-your-heart-ripped-out-of-your-chest-and-let-you-figure-out-how-to-handle-the-rest-of-your-life-without-me scenario. This particular dencuement didn't really form part of her lexicon. Once you were locked in in the eighteenth century, you really were locked in.

What's interesting is that this situation – the eighteenth-century situation – demanded a much higher level of determination and dignity in the event that things didn't go as planned than our modern free-for-all situation. In the eighteenth century you couldn't stop and start again with someone new – divorce was virtually unheard of, required a private act of parliament, and was only remotely possible to the super rich and influential. Instead, you had to cultivate your Inner Resources (otherwise known as the patchwork or coral reef of happiness), so that if life was not a bed of roses with the person you ended up with, you could still, perhaps, gain a measure of happiness and contentment. Like Charlotte Lucas, enjoying her nice house and Mr Collins-free hours. Endurance, not emotion, was the prime quality necessary for eighteenth-century marital success.

Ironically, though we live in such a different world, it's exactly these qualities that come in handy for the modern Austen heroine when you're trying to get over someone. Determination and dignity are never more important than in the aftermath of a break-up, because they may literally be the only things you have left. Cling to them like a drowning man. Likewise cling to any skerrick of restraint, reticence and rectitude you happen to possess. You think this doesn't matter. You think nothing matters anymore. But you are wrong. Things can get a lot, lot worse.

This is the story of a friend of a friend, whom I met at a dinner party. She – let's call her Lucy – broke up with her boyfriend a while ago, and she's been doing the whole pseudo-relationship friend thing. (Yes. Clearly, she had not read chapter 25 of this book.)

So. One Friday night some time ago, under the guise of 'just being friends', Lucy had called her ex to see if he wanted to meet up for a quick after-work drink. (Hah![27]) He said he was busy, but suggested that they might see each other at one of the pubs they both go to. At this point, instead of drawing the shredded garments of her Jane Austen dignity around her and going home for a good cry and some chocolate ice-cream, Lucy began a slow spiral into madness. She went to all the pubs the ex usually goes to after work: the ex wasn't at any of them. So then she took a bus, a ferry and a cab and went to the ex's flat. History does not relate how she managed to justify this to herself, but in the frenzy of the moment I'm sure she thought of something: 'I must speak to him about x'; 'I must pick up y that I left there when we were together'; 'I must reassure myself that he is not having Amazon sex with z in the living room.' Anyway, off she went.

---

27 Classic pseudo-relationship behaviour. Friday night is Date Night. So not only is Lucy signalling to the bloke that she has no-one, no-one, no-one in her life (since if she did she would, ergo, be seeing him on Date Night), but she is setting herself up for horror if he says he's busy . . . hours of wondering if he's on a date himself, and imagining him in the embrace of some Gisele Bündchen-type sex goddess. I tell you, no friendship is worth it.

Meanwhile, the ex, who had actually been telling the truth the whole time, had turned up at one of the pubs, just as he'd said he would, half an hour after Lucy had left it. (Of course, if she'd just stayed and had a quiet gin and tonic, she would have seen him there. Oh, the irony.) He was late arriving because he'd had a terrible day. He's a crown prosecutor, and he'd spent all day in court prosecuting some denizen of the criminal underworld on various charges of assault and battery. He lost the case, and the denizen walked free. To add insult to injury, the denizen then shouted at him outside the court: 'I'm going to get you, you cunt! I know where you live!' Despite being pretty hardened to the idle threats of criminals, the ex was sufficiently worried by this to ring his sister, who was staying at his flat, and tell her not to answer the door to anyone who couldn't explain themselves.

So Lucy turns up at the ex's flat at around 10 p.m. She buzzes, and the ex's sister answers. Horror for Lucy! She immediately assumes that this female voice belongs to the Amazonian sex goddess, who has wiped away the whipped cream in order to answer the speakerphone. She stands staring at the buzzer, speechless.

Horror for the sister, too! Alone in the ground-floor flat, she hears laboured breathing on the speakerphone, but no voice. The denizen of the criminal underworld immediately springs to mind, but she stays calm. She says hello a few more times, then gives up and goes back to the TV.

Lucy, meanwhile, is suddenly and entirely swamped by the World Of Pain we have already discussed. Her carefully constructed pseudo-relationship universe is crashing down around her. And, in a masochistic moment that will be familiar to many, it suddenly seems like a good idea not to make a dignified exit (quickly!!! quickly!!!), but to press forward: to Know the Worst.

At this point fate unkindly intervenes in the shape of a cheerful neighbour who recognises Lucy from the days when she was having a relationship with the ex. He opens the main door and lets Lucy in. She stands like a rabbit in the headlights in the corridor for a while. Then the masochism overwhelms her and she goes to the ex's front door and bangs on it.

Inside the flat, the sister begins to panic. She rings her brother. He listens to the story thus far: heavy breathing; banging on the door from someone clearly inside the building. He calls the police.

Meanwhile, Lucy is going into orbit out in the corridor. She's heard the woman on the speakerphone, goddammit! She knows she's in there! She bangs again. The sister cowers on the couch. Lucy goes back down the corridor and out the front door. Now fully in the grip of florid insanity, she circles the building and approaches the windows she knows are the ex's. Perhaps she will be able to see whatever there is to be seen through the window.

Let's just pause the story here for a moment and take stock. It's 10 p.m. on a Friday night, and Lucy is in the garden of her ex-boyfriend's apartment block, creeping through the undergrowth, her shoes muddy, her clothes torn, her self-respect in tatters.

How has this happened?

She has forgotten that she is a Jane Austen heroine, and she has gone completely mad, that's how.

Okay.

Moving on.

Inside the flat, the sister is also going into orbit – no surprises there. She can hear someone creeping from window to window, and the image of the denizen hurtling through the plate glass and mutilating her in vengeance against her brother is terrifyingly clear. She turns off all the lights and calls her brother again, who is by this time in a cab home to see what the matter is. Now seriously alarmed, he calls the police again.

Lucy spends the next little while – she thinks it was five minutes, maybe ten – crawling around in the undergrowth, trying and failing to catch sight of the bloke and the Amazonian en flagrante. She can see the flickering light of the television – porn! – but someone's turned the lights out – kinky! – and the rooms are in darkness. Eventually, after trying and failing to climb a tree (*Pause! A TREE!*), she goes back to the front door, where yet another unsuspecting resident – nice girl, nice business skirt, bit muddy but who is he to judge – lets her in. She goes back to the corridor. And it's here, standing outside his door, that the ex-boyfriend, closely followed by the police, find her a few minutes later.

This is a true story. Hard to believe, I know. Lucy told it with great panache, and it obviously gave her some comfort to do so: as it should. (Sometimes I think that the sole reason for undergoing horrifically embarrassing experiences is the opportunity to form them into dinner-party anecdotes. In fact, I have been known to think, even in the very middle of such experiences, that they will make good stories, and feel better as a result.)

On balance, the whole experience seemed to have sorted Lucy out a bit by the time of our dinner party; she was no longer trying to be friends with the ex, and she'd apologised to the poor sister and the police. She wasn't totally out of contact with the ex, though – she'd sent him a letter earlier that day.

When she told us this, everyone at the dinner table fell silent, and you could almost see the collective thought bubble hanging above our heads. 'What is she *doing?* How can she *still* be in touch with him after a night like that? He will have her *committed!*'

As it turns out, she was paying him back for his cab fare. When the sister rang for the second time, the ex told the cabbie he'd double the fare to get him there faster. So Lucy sent him a cheque for $120.

NOT EVERY MAN IS MR DARCY

27

I hate to say this, but every once in a very great while, our relentless search for a Jane Austen hero may lead us into error. I know, incredible thought! We have Jane as our infallible guide; we have clearly set rules and goals; we are heroines of the modern age. What could possibly go wrong? Well, ironically enough, it's our very status as heroines that imperils us.

The fact of the matter is this. The greater our focus on the quest for Mr Darcy, and the more strongly we identify with Jane and commit to the search for love, the more likely we are to discount every non-Mr Darcy man that crosses our path. We meet a nice man; we like him, he makes us laugh. But if he lacks hero potential – as, let's face it, most men do – he is ruthlessly discarded, and our heroine juggernaut rolls on.

This is absolutely okay, of course, if the man in question turns out to be a moron or a bastard. But occasionally – often, even – men who are unsuitable for any kind of hero role are nevertheless valuable additions to our lives, and if we eliminate them, we are the poorer for it.

The men we're talking about, of course, are men we could have as friends. Jane knew all about such men. She grew up among six brothers; her parents ran a small boys' boarding school at her childhood home in Hampshire; she lived in a sociable rural community. Unlike Nora Ephron in *When Harry Met Sally*, Jane completely believed in the possibility of male/female friendship. She had many male friends, whom she enjoyed talking to and writing letters about and dancing with. She understood boys – and later men: their humour and their romantic streak, their strengths and weaknesses – and felt comfortable with them. And in her novels, despite the sexual tension, conflict and drama between heroes and heroines, there's also a lot of surprisingly relaxed chat and friendly interaction. Emma Woodhouse and Mr Knightley are great mates, as are Fanny Price and Edmund Bertram, and Elinor Dashwood and Edward Ferrars. Elizabeth Bennet gets on brilliantly with her dad (you can imagine them sloping off to the pub together); Admiral and Mrs Croft and Aunt and Uncle Gardiner are not only married couples but great cronies. Men in Austen are not another species. They are different but complementary, enjoyable-for-their-own-sake human beings.

All this is relevant to us because it's easy to feel, especially as we get older, that the only way to look at men is as potential life partners. In all other ways, they become travellers from an antique land: inexplicable and mysterious, subjects of awe and fear. And this doesn't help our ability to meet them, or talk to them, or relax and have a good time with them. We can, in fact, become paralysed by the very sight of them, and by the weight of our great expectations.

If this is happening, it behoves you, as a modern Austen heroine, to take a deep breath and a step back. Stop looking at every man as a potential Mr Darcy, and think about whether he might just be a potential friend or running partner or drinking buddy. These are all totally legitimate, albeit non-hero roles, and it's good to have them in your life.

The benefits of male friends are manifold. They give you entirely different things than girlfriends do – interesting, refreshing things. For instance, men are not, generally speaking, great empathisers. Knightley is a good example: he speaks plainly to Emma, and tells her what he thinks, and what he thinks she should do; and he expects her – quite rightly – to be tough enough to take it. Unlike your girlfriends, men will not sit for hours hashing and rehashing every detail of your life. In typical Martian fashion, they will listen to your problem about the way the cute man on the bus stood up to let you sit down this morning (Did he fancy you? Did he think you were pregnant? Did he take advantage of his standing position to look down your top?), and then they will try to solve it (of course he was looking down your top; if you like him, wear a singlet tomorrow; if not, wear a turtleneck). Then they will want to move on. But in a not-at-all typical Venus fashion, this can actually be really refreshing and helpful. What John Gray MD (author, of course, of *Men are from Mars, Women are from Venus*) failed to realise is that sometimes Venusian women don't want to just endlessly talk and have Martian men endlessly listen. Sometimes problems have solutions, and Martians can figure them out, and this can be a big relief for everyone.

Men can give you a lateral approach to things. Women tend to see things in only one way. This is part of the enormous sustenance and support women give each other as friends: they work out a particular view of a situation, and then they all subscribe to it and support each other in it. Men don't do this – as rugged individualists, they come up with their own theories, which they promote with great energy, regardless of external opinion. Edmund, for example, decides Fanny needs to ride his horse for exercise, and he refuses to bow down to the combined weight of his mother and aunt (and Fanny), who have all decided that walking is quite sufficient. When Mr Darcy decides to deal with Wickham, he does so with no reference to Mr Bennet or Mr Gardiner's attempts to assist. In our own day and age, meanwhile, I was recently having a conversation with my brother, in which I was trying to talk about clothes shopping. But instead of supporting me in my frustration at the inability of crossover dresses not to gape at the neckline, he suddenly went completely off-topic. 'I want someone to make clothes out of spiders' webs,' he suddenly said, as if this was an entirely legitimate segue. 'Did you know that the tensile strength of a spider's web is, like, a hundred times greater than steel?'

Struggling to get to grips with this new topic, I nobly restrained myself from pointing out that few people require clothing with the tensile strength of steel, and anyhow, we were talking about necklines. 'How do you know this?' I asked instead.

'I don't know. How many spiders would you need, do you think, to spin enough thread for a T-shirt?' (See? Bloke, barrelling on with his theory.)

'God knows,' I said. 'You need to talk to a silkworm farmer.'

'Yes,' he agreed. 'And the problem is that you'd need to separate out the sticky from the non-sticky threads.'

'I think the stickiness is just on the round threads, not the struts. So maybe you could pick the spider off after he'd built the struts.' (Men love real-world information, unlike women – so you get kudos for actually, you know, knowing stuff.)

'Too easy!' My brother actually sounded excited, and, unable to help myself, I began to laugh. (This is another great advantage of the male conversational model: if you give them the chance, men are often very funny.) Then he said, 'No, really. People would pay a billion dollars to have the first ever piece of clothing made out of spiders' webs.'

It's not where you would ever, ever end up in a clothing conversation with a girlfriend – but sometimes, that can be a good thing.

Let me make a plea at this point for a character who, as we know, never appears in Jane Austen, but who certainly should, as a great ally of single women the world over: the gay man. Gay men inhabit, in some senses, both male and female worlds, since they appreciate and celebrate women the way other women do (in fact, sometimes far better), but still have the basis of a masculine approach to life. And because they often have fantastically high tolerances for drama, they can help all potential Austen heroines take themselves a little less seriously, and feel a little better about the ups and downs of life. The other day, for example, I was telling my lovely gay friend Hamish about what I thought was a particularly bad day at work. He listened sympathetically (as a woman would), then he stopped listening and gave me his own theory (as a man would), by recounting a day *he'd* had earlier in the week.

Hamish is an actor in a theatre company, which is just about the most romantic job in the world, except that he also has to deal with the two men who run the company, whom he likes, and who are also gay, but who are also absolutely insane.

On this particular day, the company's managing director had been acting very oddly. He'd fiddled around in the morning, and then suddenly, in the afternoon, he sacked a woman in the office for myriad crimes – crimes that Hamish couldn't discover and thought probably didn't exist. Then, less than ten minutes later, he tried to sack the tour director, despite the fact that the entire company was going on tour that very afternoon. He failed in this, because the tour director had actually resigned a few days earlier, and was working out his notice. Then two more people (*two!*) in the office resigned and three (*three!*) others tried to in protest against the first sacking. This is all in one afternoon, remember. Then, having failed to sack the tour director, the MD tried to get his car-park key off him. 'But I need it,' said the tour director.

'I don't care!' screamed the managing director.

'Well,' said the tour director, sounding weary. 'I can't start the tour unless I can get the minibus out of the car park.'

'Oh,' said the managing director. Then he screamed: 'Well, as soon as you've got the minibus out, *then* you have to give me the car-park key *immediately*!'

An hour later, the managing director had a heart attack and was rushed to hospital.

'All in all,' said Hamish at the end of the story, 'it was a really weird day.' And it made me feel so much better about mine.

So there you go. Male friends. Solving problems, offering lateral points of view, cheering you up. Valuable roles all three. There are only two final points to make; points you no doubt know, but that Jane wants to remind you of.

1 YOUR MEN FRIENDS WILL HAVE FRIENDS

And while you may not fancy your male friends, you may fancy *their* friends. How many Mr Darcys are lurking behind Bingleys the world over? As Helen Reddy pointed out: numbers too big to ignore. So, just as Mrs Bennet explains how the Jane/Bingley connection will throw her younger daughters 'in the way of *other* rich men', so knowing non-heroic boys will throw you into the paths of *other*, potentially heroic boys.

2 SOMETIMES FRIENDSHIPS CHANGE

You know, weirder things have happened. Sometimes you have a lovely buddy, and, just like Emma and Knightley, the two of you adore hanging out and talking and making each other laugh, but you resolutely do not fancy each other. (Or, more usually, you don't fancy him: it's usually the case that even in happy platonic friendships the man thinks the woman is a bit of alright.) Alas, of course, with this particular hypothetical friend, there isn't a skerrick of Darcy-frisson about him; you've probably even tried to set him up with your friends on the basis that such a lovely man should not be wasted, and he might have done the same for you. Meanwhile, the Mr Darcy search rages on, and you get so busy Standing Still and Smiling and going on Drink Dates that you don't see lovely friend for a while. And during this period he joins a gym and gets his hair cut and loses his entire wardrobe in a forest fire, so that next time you meet up he's wearing army-surplus store fatigues and a plain navy T-shirt through which you can see visible pecs and some kind of corrugation where his beer belly used to be. And as he pushes the pub door open, sees you and gives you a big grin, you suddenly glimpse a cravat pin beneath the navy-blue cotton. Welcome to the best of all possible worlds.

A BRILLIANT CAREER

28

Sometimes, in the white heat of finding-Mr-Darcy fever, it's hard to care about your career. In what possible way can dragging yourself out of bed every morning to be beaten black and blue by the brutal public-transport system, your brutal boss, and the whole brutal mercantile world be compared to finding a six foot man with broad shoulders and a nice line in silk waistcoats? Working, frankly, seems a waste of time.

Big mistake, says Jane Austen. Not because the women in her novels are career girls – far from it. The women of her time – and in her novels – had little other recourse in life but marriage. 'Marriage had always been her object', she writes of Charlotte Lucas in *Pride and Prejudice*. 'It was the only honourable provision for well-educated young women of small fortune.' Unless, like Emma Woodhouse, you were independently wealthy, you had no choice: marry or burn.

Well, *apparently* no choice. In fact, women in Jane Austen *do* work. Emma's own governess, the beloved Mrs Weston (Miss Taylor that was), has been a working woman all Emma's life (looking after Emma, which must indeed have been hard labour at times); Jane Fairfax is facing a similar future for most of the novel. Of course, *she* views it as a fate worse than death – she compares it to the slave trade – but this, you can't help feeling, is a reflection on Jane Fairfax in particular (who is lovely but, let's face it, a bit highly strung and sensitive for most tastes) rather than on working women in general. One of Jane Austen's close friends, Anne Sharp, was a governess at her brother Edward's home. Jane kept in touch with her throughout her various postings (she ended up, rather brilliantly, running her own successful girls' school in Liverpool, 'a clever, rather dominant woman', much loved by the community), and after her death Cassandra sent her a lock of Jane's hair and thirty pounds.

And not every female job in Jane's novels *is* in fact bad. Look, once again, at Mrs Weston. She is not only beloved by Emma and her father, but has managed, while being a working woman, to meet and marry the cheerful, kind, rich Mr Weston. By the end of the novel she's even had a baby. She's got it all going on, girlfriend, and she is loving her life.

Admittedly, for most women, life as a career girl in the eighteenth century was no bed of roses. (And what has changed?, I hear you cry.) Being a governess or a lady's companion – about the only options open to gentlewomen – could, if you ended up in the wrong place or with the wrong family, be one long nightmare of small incorrigible children, patronising employers and fighting off the family's spotty teenage sons (not to mention their gouty goatish fathers) in the corridors of the east wing.

But what would you rather? Life as a white slave with three little children racing around shouting and biting each other, as Jane Fairfax is contemplating, or *Mr Collins* as your *husband*, running your life and making a continuous, wearying fool of himself and *getting into bed with you at night?*

The point Jane wants to make is that a bad marriage is far, far worse than a bad job. If the feckless and foolish Frank Churchill had not pulled his finger out in time, and Jane Fairfax *had* become a governess, it would have been horrible, granted, for someone of her temperament. But she would have kept her friends, she would have kept her honour, she would have remained a functioning member of society. She could have moved to a new job with no loss of face if it had been completely unbearable and tried again. Compare such a woman – her self-respect and, largely, her social standing intact – to Maria Bertram in *Mansfield Park*. Married to the impenetrably stupid Rushworth and clearly feeling that life is insupportable, Maria leaves him and runs away with Henry Crawford. And as a result, her life is *over*. She cannot be received by her friends, family or acquaintances; she is cut off, wiped out, erased from the rollcall of the civilised world. This, you could argue, is the ultimate consequence of a bad marriage. A bad job is far better than that.

In our own work, in our own day and age, Jane doesn't need us to be thrusting and ambitious. We don't have to be heaving ourselves hand over fist up the greasy pole of corporate success, leaving carnage in our wake. Essentially, she just wants us to maintain our dignity and independent spirit, like any good Jane Austen heroine.

Jane herself was a great pragmatist, and in this regard, too, work is good, because usually nobody at work cares, quite frankly, about you or your tormented private life: they just want you to do what you're paid for and keep quiet about everything else. Harsh as it sounds, Jane would regard this as a positive thing. Something about the discipline of getting up every day, going out into the world, and contributing your mite to the turning of the great wheel of commerce is good for the psyche and the soul.

There's also the minor detail that work can be deeply fantastic. If you are lucky enough to find something you love doing, work can bring you not only a wage, but also real happiness and satisfaction. And in this sense it becomes a major piece in your patchwork of happiness: right up there with getting your hair blow-dried and borrowing your new library books each Saturday morning. And in bad times, it becomes a comfort and a consolation. When everything else in your life is going to hell in a hand basket – as it periodically does, in even the best-regulated heroine's world – it can be a relief to think to yourself, 'Well, at least work's okay.' Plus, people who have jobs they love are deeply attractive. Think how lovely – and unusual – it is to hear someone talking with real enthusiasm about their work. It makes you want to hang out with them, to inveigle yourself into their job-enjoying world.

Having a job you actually like, of course, is a privilege – but it's one you can actively pursue. If you hate your job, change it. Think hard about what you love doing, and try to do it for a career. In this respect, money is far less important than enjoyment. The happy check-out chick who really loves restacking the aisles and gets a big kick out of working those terrifying rotary-saw things at the deli counter is far better off in the self-respect/happiness stakes than the disaffected head of an international bank.

There are lots of ways of getting a job you love. You can study for new qualifications; get a bank loan and start a business; or answer the ad for a curator for the Keats museum in Rome at the foot of the Spanish Steps that provides a one-bedroom flat on-site in the listed nineteenth-century building with a view over the Eternal City.[28] It doesn't

---

28 This was a real ad for a real job that I found once. And no, I did not apply. I know. It pains me every day.

matter if you're not a curator, speak no Italian and have never heard about seasons of mist or Grecian urns. It's not, in this sense, about getting the job at all. It's about expanding your field of possibilities.

In this regard, my friend Ann has a fantastic career-based theory that she calls Future Friday. This theory is based on the demoralising reality that even when you actively hate your job, you don't usually have a lot of time to do anything about it, because most of your productive daylight hours are actually taken *up* with your job. This means you're in a kind of catch-22 situation. Of course you tell yourself that you will write applications early in the morning, look on seek.com late at night and send your CV off in your lunch hour, but in fact all this is bloody hard to organise, and so usually you don't do any of it, and then you feel a terrible failure – which in turn means you're even *less* likely to do anything about it next week.

Enter Future Friday. It's very straightforward: you simply let yourself off the hook Monday through Thursday, when you are flat out just keeping your head above water. And then on Friday – every Friday – you do *one* positive thing towards changing your life. Voila!

Of course, it may take several Fridays to get things moving – but just think how long it took Jane to get a novel published. She wrote the first draft of *Pride and Prejudice* when she was twenty: it was eventually published the year she turned thirty-eight. *Sense and Sensibility* had a sixteen-year gap between first draft and publication; *Northanger Abbey*, twenty.

One final point. Worthwhile men respect working women. Be suspicious of a man who says things like 'No woman of mine's going to work.' To which you might reply: 'Why not? Because you'll be dragging a wildebeest back to the cave each night before you club her with your mammoth bone?' Clearly, such a man's got some ego issues to work through, and you don't want to be around while he fights his way out of his loin cloth and into the twenty-first century.

MONEY ISN'T EVERYTHING
29

Money matters. We all know this, and Jane did too. (For most of her life she existed on an allowance of fifty pounds a year – roughly £1600 in today's money – which was no picnic.) And this informs our search for Mr Darcy in an unexpected way. That is, we all hope he is going to be terrifically rich. It is a somewhat embarrassing but self-evident truth that none of us, in our wildest fantasies of masculine perfection, imagine a man who is six foot two, chisel-jawed, deeply kind to small animals and children (and us) and also poor as a church mouse.

Jane understood the appeal of a financially secure hero. Mr Knightley, Captain Wentworth and Colonel Brandon are all solidly well off; Mr Darcy is loaded; even Edmund Bertram and Edward Ferrars are comfortably established. Indeed, poor men like Willoughby and Wickham are disqualified from hero status altogether (though poverty is, of course, not their only failing).

In Jane's day, there was a very practical reason for the hero having money, which was that broke couples could not marry, and since gentlewomen rarely worked (or if they did, they got paid hardly anything), the responsibility to be cashed up fell squarely on men. This is why Jane's sister Cassandra couldn't marry her curate Tom, and why he went off to the West Indies and perished – he went, alas, in pursuit not only of souls but filthy lucre. Even closer to home, it may well have been the reason Jane and Tom Lefroy were so swiftly separated: Tom Lefroy was poor, from a large family of siblings, and reliant on a rich relative; everybody knew that the family fortunes, quite literally, depended on him. Marrying a similarly penniless girl, however cheeky and charming, didn't form part of anybody's plan – probably not even his.

Despite this rather grim impact on her life, Jane remained pretty hardnosed about the need for a competence: as a realist, she understood why it was necessary. Of course, she doesn't advocate marrying for money, nor does she regard an overt obsession with money as acceptable – the grasping Fanny Dashwood is appalling in her naked greed. Nor is Jane a Marianne Dashwood sympathiser. Jane would never declare, as Marianne does: 'Money can only give happiness where there is nothing else to give it . . . It can afford no real satisfaction.' She would be off in a corner, quietly doing the sums on the back of an envelope. She knew that someone, somewhere in a relationship needs to have some cash.

But, in a radical departure from the conventions of her day, Jane does not believe that someone necessarily has to be the man. Certainly not. Look at Emma: she could have married whomever she liked, as long as he was a gentleman. Jane has three suggestions for getting money into our lives, and Emma falls into option number one: being born with it. This option is lovely and straightforward, but Jane knows it's unusual: Emma is her only heroine who grows up independently wealthy. The second option, of course, is for a heroine to marry money, as Elizabeth Bennet so spectacularly does, as do most of her other heroines to a greater or lesser degree. And the third – and most relevant to our particular deliberations – is to earn the cold hard cash ourselves. Which is exactly what Jane did. She earnt, according to her carefully kept records, a total of £684 13s from the four of her novels that were published in her lifetime – a little over £23,000 in today's money – which is pretty appalling, even for that most-maligned of wage earners, the poor author. (Ahem.) But she also invested 600 pounds in the Navy Five Per Cents, which brought her an additional income of thirty pounds a year, out of which she was able to buy luxuries and fripperies and, often, gifts for her family and friends.

Earning our own money can be harder to get our heads around than one might expect. As we've already acknowledged, however V-for-victory, black-power-salute we are about women's independence, most of us start out by believing that, at some point, Mr Darcy is simply going to roll into town, dripping banknotes, and solve our money worries with one sweep of his well-manicured (yet impossibly manly) hand. I remember having coffee with a lovely friend one day – a Harvard-educated Princeton academic – who announced that she had just been to see a financial planner. She was in her early thirties, and when I asked her how it had gone, she said in tones of wonder: 'It was pretty interesting. I realised that until this moment, my financial planning for the future has involved the sole strategy of meeting a really rich man.'

There are two crucial points here: 1) really rich men are depressingly thin on the ground. (You may have noticed this phenomenon yourself.) And 2) even if you find one, his money is still his money. It doesn't matter how many children you bear him or houses you decorate for him or yachts you sail around the Mediterranean with him, he who signs the cheques has the power. Charlotte Lucas has no power. Nor does Jane Fairfax, once foolish (but financially secure) Frank Churchill prances back onto the scene. And if we translate these women into our own time, the heroine who has taken her eye off the ball at work and is earning a piss-weak pittance because she's relying on a man to come along and take care of all things financial has correspondingly little power. A woman, however, who has gritted her teeth, put in the hard yards and got herself a decent job, with decent conditions and a decent wage, can do whatever the hell she likes, with a man or without him. I want to spend $300 getting my hair cut – and goddammit, I *can*! Because I answer to no man about my money.

Money in Jane's world is a facet of every heroine's self-respect. Earning your own money, living your own life – paying your rent or mortgage; managing a budget (even if it's a kind of okay-bank-balance-zero-two-minute-noodles-from-now-till-next-week budget); feeding and clothing and entertaining yourself with the fruits of your own labour – none of this is to be taken lightly. It's a fundamental building block of any heroine's self-confidence and healthy ego.

And as such, it means that a financially self-reliant heroine is far less likely to be pushed around by a man than her dependent equivalent. At the risk of sounding like an ad for a government social-work initiative, economic independence is one of the best insurances against physical or emotional abuse – in the eighteenth century and today.

One other small point: heroes do not like gold diggers. I have male friends who remark with horror about girls who gently bring the conversation around to property portfolios within five minutes of a first meeting. Clause four of Jonesy and Macca's Chamonix declaration read (and I quote): 'No more princesses.'[29] No heroine should ever have to ask questions about her potential hero's finances, because a heroine can financially take care of herself. And thus, her search for true love remains unsullied by mercenary calculations.

So, how can we all attract a bit more money into our lives? (Apart, of course, from the tried-and-true methods of either winning the lottery or asking the universe.) Well mostly, once again, via our Brilliant Careers. Look at your career, and ask yourself this question: am I earning enough for what I do? Women – even Jane Austen heroines – are notoriously hopeless at asking for pay rises, seeking promotion and, basically, telling their bosses how great they are. Men, meanwhile, do all these things, all day long. Thus women tend to stagnate in the salary stakes while men snap up the promotions and financial rewards. So stand up for yourself, sister! Find out how much other people at your level at work are earning. If it's less than you, it's time you looked for a promotion. If it's more, make an appointment with your boss, go in with your hand on your hip and state your case for a pay rise.

---

[29] Translation: princesses are girls who look good and want to go out with (read marry) high-powered executive types for the sole reason that they are high-powered executives. Both Jonesy and Macca, of course, *are* high-powered executives, so this is a constant danger for them.

This is hard, I acknowledge. It's even harder if you're in a relationship and you already earn more than your boyfriend: it's easy to feel you don't deserve, somehow, to earn more than he does. But hang in there. Never feel embarrassed about your excellent job or excellent wage. Never apologise. This is the career equivalent of dumbing yourself down. Any man worth his salt – any modern-day Mr Darcy, even one who himself lives in penury – will love and respect you for it.

In the unlikely event you're already milking your job for every penny it's worth, think about money management. I know, I know: a phrase to strike terror into the heart of even the most mercenary of heroines. But it doesn't have to. You don't have to suddenly spring forth upon an astonished world as a fully-fledged financial guru, trading derivatives, predicting the interest rate and playing the currency markets. For starters, just set up a savings account. Look for one with high interest, but don't even worry about that too much – just get one into which you can make a direct debit every week from your main account,[30] and *one that you cannot access from an automatic teller*. Then set up a sum to be automatically transferred each week.

---

30 Watch out for bank charges. Don't get any account that charges you fees; and don't set up any direct debits that involve a transfer fee. Jane hates paying bank fees, and so do we.

Once you're underway with a minimum amount, you may even decide to, you know, sacrifice something in your day-to-day life in order to save more. This, I acknowledge, is not much fun (though there can be a bizarre kind of satisfaction watching your bank balance rise: like Scrooge watching his pile of gold grow. It makes you feel like rubbing your hands and cackling, '$1000! $2000! $5000. *Ye-ha-ha-ha!!!*'). I remember having a conversation with my friend Lenny about this when she was on a diet as well as a strict savings plan. We were talking about how her local council had just begun a recycling programme. As she put it: 'So those are my rules for life at the moment. Don't eat anything; don't buy anything; don't throw anything away.' Not much fun on the face of it, but in actual fact, quite enjoyable in a blitz-spirit, can-I-survive-another-week-on-a-tin-of-beans-and-a-heel-of-parmesan way.

So just get started. Even if you're only saving ten bucks. I used to think this was ridiculous. Ten bucks? The point at which such piddling sums could ever amount to anything useful seemed so far in future as to be entirely pointless. 'I know,' my Dad told me. 'But one day the future arrives.' And it really does. So brace yourself, take a deep breath, and investigate your bank balance.

LIFE WITHOUT A MR DARCY
30

Is there life without Mr Darcy? At the end of all this discussion, which has been aimed specifically at finding Mr Darcy and binding him to your side until the end of life as we know it, this may seem like a strange, pessimistic question. But it's worth asking, nevertheless. Does Jane Austen – and by extension do we, as her heroines – believe that life can go on, even if our hero never appears?

The answer is simple. Yes. Absolutely. In this (as in so many things), Jane is profoundly modern. Her heroines – unlike many of the female characters of eighteenth-century literature – have options other than men. Sometimes not very desirable options, it's true, but options nonetheless. None of them will be cast out of their homes if they remain single; all have families who value them as companions and carers. This might not be a very exciting or expansive fate – but it was, after all, Jane's own, and look what she achieved from within its narrow confines. Some heroines, in fact, actually prefer the unmarried life – Emma certainly does (though we know how long *that* lasts). And all of them feel that remaining unmarried, and thus in some essential sense free and independent, is better than yoking their fate to someone they do not love.

This is the crux of the Jane Austen heroine: she is psychologically whole. This is a hard concept to explain, but you can see it in these women – and in Jane herself. Even at their most despairing, there's a sense of undamaged selfhood to them: a sense of wholeness and peace that characters like Lydia Bennet, Maria Bertram, Isabella Thorpe and Mary Crawford don't have. Think about this group of girls: think about what they've had to do, psychologically, to make sense of their lives with Wickham and Rushworth et al. They've had to fundamentally deceive themselves. Lydia has had to convince herself that Wickham loves her; Maria that Henry Crawford will take care of her; Isabella that she never wanted Captain Tilney anyhow; Mary Crawford that she can do far better than Edmund Bertram. In other words, they have to convince themselves of something they know to be a lie. Our heroines don't have to fight this ugly internal battle. Even when all seems lost, they're still able to be truthful to the world, and – far more importantly – to themselves.

It's not that meeting Mr Darcy isn't the desirable end of the singledom road. As Jane acknowledges, ending up with a lovely man you really adore is a brilliantly good outcome, in that day or this. The marriage of true minds is a fantastic, comforting, extraordinary thing; and there is nothing like loving someone, and them loving you back, as a basis for a happy life.

But it's not the only basis. Happiness, as we've already discussed, is a many splendoured thing, and it's not achievable only through marriage. For proof of this, once again, we have only to look to Jane's own life. No, she never married. But is it possible she could have been happier than when her books began to gain recognition? Happier than when her celebrity began to build, even slightly, and the money began to come in, even slightly, and influential people began to talk about her, even slightly? (And sometimes not so slightly: the Prince Regent himself enjoyed her novels so much he requested she dedicate one to him: *Emma* is the result. One of her favourites among her own novels, dedicated to a fat man she didn't really care for, but still. The Prince Regent!) Jane's books brought her extraordinary happiness. A different happiness than Tom Lefroy might have brought her, true – but who's to say which is better? Who's to say, given the choice, she might not have chosen fictional Fitzwilliam over real-life Tom?

And this is the key thing to remember about the hunt for a soulmate. What you are really hunting for is happiness. That's what Mr Darcy – and every one of Jane's heroes – represents: he is the living, breathing, many-caped personification of a happy life. And this is both a great truth and a trick of the light. A truth, because, as we've discussed already, there is nothing like falling in love to bring you undeserved joy. But it's also a trick, because no man, at the end of the day, can make you happy. No man, no marriage, no country estate or wardrobe of flower-imprinted dresses or fleet of servants at your beck and call. In the end, the only person that can bring you happiness, Ms Heroine, is you.

So do your best in pursuit of Mr Darcy. Seek him here, seek him there, seek him like the Frenchies seek him: everywhere. But be alert to the fact that what you're really seeking is happiness. And if you find it en route, in some way other than through marriage to an Austen hero, don't let it pass you by.

And at this point, the task of this book is done. Let the real-life game begin!

ACKNOWLEDGEMENTS

I want to thank my publisher, Ingrid Ohlsson, for coming to me with the idea for this book, and making the writing process so much fun. Deb Callahan, my agent, has been truly generous with her time and expertise, and my editor, Emma Rafferty, has borne several hundred manual manuscript changes with great humour and professionalism. Charlotte Ree has been a PR dynamo, and Allison Colpoys did a magical job on the cover.

Thanks to all my editors, past and present, for giving me great stories, caring about words, and encouraging me to care about them too. And thanks to all the subs at *Good Weekend*: the unsung heroes who make stories better.

Thanks to Mum and Dad for proving that relationships can last, and to Martine for being there through the many, many years that form the bedrock of this book. And thank you to Dom for his never-failing calm, intelligence and kindness, not to mention his crumbless expertise in the kitchen.

And thank you, finally, to all the people whose stories appear in these pages. Some of their names have been changed, some are no longer single, and one has been recently convinced that the answer to the meaning of life does not, in fact, lie in the neatness of one's drawer dividers. But they are still my people, and I owe them. They know who they are.